C000125881

PULPI. ,

PULPIT
JOURNEYS

Edited by Geoffrey Stevenson

DARTON·LONGMAN+TODD

First published in 2006 by
Darton, Longman and Todd Ltd
1 Spencer Court
140–142 Wandsworth High Street
London SW18 4JJ

Compilation © 2006 Geoffrey Stevenson

The right of Geoffrey Stevenson to be identified as
the Compiler of this work has been asserted in accordance
with the Copyright, Designs and Patents Act 1988.

ISBN 0–232–52617–6

A catalogue record for this book is available from the British Library.

Acknowledgement
Poems by C. S. Lewis copyright © C. S. Lewis Pte Ltd, 1964.
Extract on p. 107 reprinted by permission.

Phototypeset by Intype, London
Printed and bound in Great Britain by
Page Bros, Norwich, Norfolk

Contents

Foreword

I tried speed reading this manuscript but couldn't! I was arrested by the human stories and slowed down to think about my own pulpit journey and, more important, my own relationship with God. These pages may not be the most elegant literature but they are powerful descriptions that you cannot gainsay. Richard Bewes traces his family history in a way that made me shiver at the sense of God's hand and God's voice in his call to preach the Gospel, Mike Breen's dyslexic journey shows that the brokenness of the preacher is the cracked pot that leaks life-giving water. Steve Chalke offers practical advice as a communicator who travels comfortably to and from studio and pulpit. Ian Coffey believes that passion is central to preaching, which is 'bringing truth through personality'.

James Dunn, one of our leading New Testament theologians, steps out of his academic gown to reveal the intimate details of how he prepares to preach. Susan Durber made me want to order immediately all five books about preaching that had made such an impact on her, and to tell her that her grandmother's prophecy shows every sign of coming true! Joel Edwards underscores a reprise in these chapters that the call to preach comes to young people and children.

Faith Forster has four questions with which she engages as she wrestles with the text, the people, the spirit and the time! Roger Forster writes as he preaches, with the zeal and the appeal of the evangelist. Rob Frost has Jesus at the heart of his preaching; far from being culturally irrelevant he shows how story-based oratory lies at the heart of our culture. And just when you think that all these preachers come from one particular stable, out strides Leslie Griffiths – for five years Donald Soper's understudy at Hyde Park Corner, and an advocate of the seamlessness of the social and spiritual Gospel.

Andy Hawthorne takes you to the front line of rapping and texting the Gospel. Anthony Reddie shows how Black theology has recovered the power of 'captivating narrative' and jazz-like interactive proclamation which sees the improvisation of the preacher connecting the fixity of the text with the fluidity of the context. Simon Vibert shows his aspiration to preach in such a way 'that the solemn attention of the whole audience is riveted'. David Wilkinson proves how, although it may be given to an individual to preach, preaching is a gift to, for and with the whole community.

Reading all these contributions has brought my own preaching under fresh scrutiny. Preachers are always accountable to the community and to God, but rarely do we risk the opportunity of letting others evaluate our effectiveness. Rarely do we hear others preaching, especially those of a different tradition and culture.

This book made me remember that I wrote my first sermon when I was a child. It was on the importance of closing your eyes when saying your prayers! I can't remember what I said or why I did it! But I was struck by these pulpit journeys which trace the call back to childhood. It suggests that the formation of the preacher is a greater task in the purposes of God than we realise and certainly predates formal theological education. If the formation begins before, it certainly should continue beyond the certification.

There is much to learn from these fellow travellers and preachers and more to be said than is contained in these essays. Over and above the Scriptures, the writings of the Church Fathers and many biographies, there are two particular pieces that have disciplined me in my own preaching.

The first is an essay by George Orwell from *Inside the Whale* about politics and the English language. It is a must for all preachers. He accuses politicians of lazily using stale and repetitive images that lack freshness and originality. You can read this criticism word for word about the way many of us who preach lapse into clichés and well-worn metaphors. Forgive me, there are even some on these pages! But don't let that put you off! Let's learn how to preach with fresh and original phrases and images.

The second is the advice that Lloyd George gave to the young Harold Macmillan about how to give a speech in the House of Commons. It is full of riveting wisdom and concludes with 'Never forget the value of the pause'. His lessons in oratory served Macmillan well throughout his political career. The same lessons would benefit many preachers.

In St Paul's famous letter of 1 Corinthians 13 he is translated as saying, 'Now we see through a glass darkly'. He said no such thing! Rather, he wrote, 'Now we see through the glass in an enigma'. In other words, we do not have the language of heaven to communicate the mysteries of God and the Gospel, all we have to communicate the truth is parable, allegory, simile, metaphor and story. This was the method that Jesus himself used. Time and again in this book you will hear the preachers tell you about the importance of story in preaching and teaching the Christian faith. It is the story that engages the mind and the heart and reaches the will through our emotions. That's the power of a good story. That's the power of the Good News. That's the power of preaching.

The Right Reverend James Jones
Bishop of Liverpool

Preface

As merely the editor of this collection, I claim no credit at all for the wise and inspiring words generously – and humbly – contributed to this book by the fifteen preachers here. They have done the hard work, not only in crafting these essays on their formative influences as preachers, but in the hard graft of preaching itself. Year after year, in earnest prayer and diligent Bible study, standing up obediently before the faithful and the faithless, often without any confidence save in the God who saves, they have collected the experience and earned the right to write here.

The idea for this book came while I was Director of the Centre for Christian Communication at St John's College in Durham. Established in 1996 as a research and training institute for church leaders and ministry students, and owing much to the Principal of the College, David Day, its vision was for effective church communication and the renewal of biblical preaching in the context of our mass-media-saturated culture. Years of conferences, courses, training events and research projects were made possible through contributions and generous grants from many individuals and trusts, but particular mention should be made of the Jerusalem Trust, the William Leech Charity and the Garfield Weston Foundation. I thank especially the Sir Halley Stewart Trust, whose specific and generous funding of the Centre's VOX Project in 2004 and 2005 enabled the production of this book to take place.

Encouragement and help have been also freely given to me personally. I shall no doubt embarrass David Day by mentioning him again, but his kindness, gentle direction, support and faith have been incomparable. David Wilkinson, as Associate Director of the Centre as well as Fellow in Christian Apologetics at St John's College, has been a fine colleague, a warm friend, and sterling conversation partner in the planning of this and many other projects. Steve Croft, while Warden of Cranmer Hall at St John's College, gave support and direction, wise counsel and continual encouragement. Stephen Wright of the College of Preachers has shared in a number of projects with me and we are at work on another. I am grateful to James Cook and Amabel Craig for their work on the VOX Project. Most especially, I honour and thank Judith, my utterly lovely, wise and insightful wife. She has listened with me to many preachers from far and wide (and knows a good sermon when she hears it), assisted with the text of this book, and most wonderfully of all, has for 27 years sought with me to worship and to serve God and to build up the church in whatever modest ways have been open to us.

To him be all glory and praise.

Geoffrey Stevenson
New College, Edinburgh

Introduction

How do you make a good preacher?

First, you take a message, burning inside a man or woman who has an intimate relationship with God and an understanding of the ways of God, then mix it with an extensive knowledge of Scripture and the writings of Church Fathers, blend in a profound understanding of doctrine and systematic theology with a good grasp of science and psychology, season with a twinkle in the eye and a gift for storytelling …

No, that wasn't the question. Those are the ingredients, possibly the make-up or maybe the constituents of a good preacher. My question is about process. How to form – produce/generate/train – a good preacher? How does the preacher gain or come by those qualities? This is a more difficult question, and cooking metaphors will not serve.

Voice training and public-speaking practice; memorising Bible verses, lectures on sermon construction; master-apprentice relationship, comparing notes with other preachers, hearing great preaching; reading the classics of literature, steeping oneself in modern novels or listening to radio broadcasters; knowing the congregation, their needs and their questions; seeking God in prayer and fasting, praying with 'the Bible in one hand and a newspaper in the other' … Will these do it? Perhaps. But still: in which order, to what degree, at which stage of development and by whose provision? Are all of these – are any of these – necessary for all preachers? Can a person develop into an outstanding preacher without any of these? It is not unknown. Rules are hard to find.

What is a good preacher, anyway? Our answer to that will affect the kind of training we prescribe. Is it one who unfailingly draws a crowd, packs out the church or (in some tele-evangelist-cluttered broadcasting future) boosts the viewing figures? Or is it the preacher who gives her congregation a varied diet of teaching, exhortation, correction, reproof, encouragement and inspiration? Indeed, what is a good sermon? But now we are way beyond the provenance of this brief introduction.

A couple of assumptions

Before looking at what we can do to become or to train better preachers, there are two assumptions I make. The first is that a sermon hasn't been preached until it has been heard. Sermon notes or even a full script do not make a sermon; a sermon is what happens when the listeners 'come to the party'.

The second assumption is even more fundamental: unless God shows up, nobody's going to have a good time at the party. Sound scriptural exegesis, fine words, fancy rhetoric, moving stories and powerful argument, receptive listeners, awake and attentive – none of these will guarantee that the Word of God is preached and heard. There is a sovereign act of the Spirit of God that we can often quench but never command.

There are implications for preachers that arise from these assumptions. A great preacher may not be attended to by great numbers, but she or he will have highly attentive listeners, listeners who will probably have already experienced God's word through a mouthpiece chosen and favoured by him. They bring expectation, they bring hunger and thirst, and they bring their need for consolation and encouragement, for teaching and instruction. They 'would see Jesus'. They show that they are ready to have their lives transformed by Christ and to be 'not hearers of the word only, but doers'. Storytellers often quote the maxim: 'There are ears that have the power to open mouths.' Good preachers can only exist where there are good listeners. If we wish to see better preachers in the land, we must also wish – pray – that there are more churches in the land with at least a remnant of people who hunger for the nourishment, the energy and excitement, the healing, and the life of the *kerygma* of Jesus Christ as it comes to us in the word of God. Preaching is not the only way to present Christ, but it is still one of the most important ways.

Who are these people?

I guess, unless you are an inveterate church-hopping sermon taster, it is unlikely that you will have listened to and seen more than a few of the preachers writing here. There is a broad spectrum of churchmanship and theology that forms the background to this group, and that has been intentional. Unless you are worshipping on Mars, however, if you have not actually heard them, you should have heard *of* a fair sample of the men and women here. Nearly all of them are well-known for their preaching in the church circles in which they move, and between them have preached many thousands of sermons. We will have to wait for a multi-media reprint of this book to include recorded video samples of each of them preaching.

If you are unfamiliar with *all* of these names, or if (as is more likely) you are shocked by the omission of some obvious names, I can only beg your apology. I have sought to be as catholic as possible and to seek contributions from across the theological and cultural spectrum. I wish there were more women. When a woman preaches, she often enables me to hear God speaking in, as I hope you would expect, different but complementary ways. I wish there were more Roman Catholics. The homily within the Mass and as a preparation for the eucharistic act has particular qualities of revelation that do not always appear in discursive expositions eight or ten times the length. Most of all, I wish

simply that there were a greater number of preachers writing
here, simply because each preacher, and the way God has called
and formed them, is unique. This is so, just as each sermon-event
is unique, a never-to-be-repeated congruence of a preacher,
Spirit-inspired preparation, a congregation, and the Word that
God desires to speak to those hearers at that particular time.
More preachers writing here would have meant more delightful
stories, more powerful testimonies to the grace and mercy of
God, and more insight into the fascinating and vital process of
shaping a preacher. But a book, like a sermon, should be the right
length and no longer, and should end before the reader starts
looking at the clock.

This book is a collection of individual stories. Here we want to
explore how good preachers have learned and developed – at
least to read about their understanding of their development,
and in their own words. Prominent preachers in the UK were
asked to write or to talk freely about the formative influences on
their preaching. They responded generously, and have written
with honesty and passion.

Preachers – most good preachers – are not much given to
revealing themselves from the pulpit. Modesty prevails, but also
they have learned not to talk about their own prayer life, suffer-
ings, extensive reading or adorable children. That is usually
distracting at best, and at worst a misuse of the power of their
position. As David Day remarks, when preaching crosses over
the line to exhibitionism, with too much raw and embarrassing
emotion, 'half the congregation want to flee the building and the
other half want to give the preacher therapy'.[1] So it may be sur-
prising to hear preachers in such confessional mode. Indeed, it
took quite a lot of arm-twisting to wrest such revelations from
them. But there is considerable value in such autobiographical
detail.

I have to say that in soliciting these essays, it was sometimes
very hard to keep these preachers from preaching, as they shared
their stories. I hope you will forgive them that. It is in the blood.
It is what they do. And for the studious reader there is much to

be learned from the didactic passages, for the words of wisdom derive from experience and reflection. The stories also have their way of teaching, and that has been the aim of the book. What is encouraging is the way common themes have emerged from a wide range of individuals with very different stories to tell. One conclusion I begin to draw is that the influence of the practice of many faithful 'unsung heroes' has as much place in the formation of a preacher as do particular mentors and teachers. Also, we see here again and again that at the heart of preaching there is story-telling: storytelling that invites the listener to make connections and to see how their story, God's story and the story of their community interact and are the locus for the work of the Holy Spirit.

We see, I think, that forming starts early, and that good and attentive mentors and models are crucial to the development of many preachers. We also see again and again that there is urgency, passion, a compulsion, something outside of normal egoism or vain ambition, that drives preachers to the pulpit. This powerful, sometimes unshakeable urge to share the word of God is usually mixed with humility and something reticent, some-thing reminding the preachers of their unworthiness, it seems, to take on the task. They also realise, in particular, the sovereign role God plays in all the aspects of the sermon-event, from the preacher's prayer and study to the listener's reception of a life-changing word. Finally, patterns (if not rules) begin to emerge, showing us why one is called and not another. Holiness, wisdom, learning, oratory skills are usually perceived more by listeners and congregations than by the possessor of these attributes. The preacher, in all humility, may doubt, but to the listener, it is often crystal clear that God has called, touched, empowered ...

Conclusion

If you are a preacher, I hope through this book you will take time to reflect on your own preaching journey. I have done so – and found to my amusement that almost all the preachers influencing me have been named David: such as Watson, MacInnes, Day and Wilkinson.[2]

If you are not a preacher, I hope this book will act as a small challenge and inspiration to the way you listen to preachers. They are involved, on many levels, in the message they are trying to deliver. God does not use his faithful preachers as automatons or robotic mouthpieces. Their words are authenticated by the integrity of the lives they lead and by their passion for knowing God and helping others to know God. See – as well as listen to – the whole man or woman who has been called to preach, and you will, I believe, see and hear God more clearly.

Few of us would claim to have a recipe that will unfailingly produce outstanding sermons, and fewer still would say there are universal rules to make a good preacher. Compounding the challenge, preaching is so often a solo activity: finding the message in prayerful seclusion, refining it in concentrated study, delivering it to blank faces, receiving well-meaning but unrevealing comments afterwards. All too often the isolation inevitably felt by any public speaker becomes normative for the whole process. The results can be seen in so many of our churches: there is a low expectation of the sermon from congregation and minister alike; preachers find extreme difficulty in improving, or in making changes to their pattern and style; and preaching teams do not complement (and seldom compliment) one another.

This collection of essays and interviews is an effort to reverse that trend. It is stab at initiating dialogue, a way of fostering collaboration, and an attempt to share models of good practice. It is a declaration that we are not alone in this sometimes terrifying, sometimes exhilarating vocation. Like a cloud of witnesses, these preachers testify that we are not alone in this work. Above all, they convey again and again, that God has been with them, from hearing the word, through living with and refining the word, to making possible the reception of the word. God is in every attempt to preach faithfully in his name. Let the preachers in these pages describe some of the ways they have experienced that grace and that precious presence.

NOTES

1. David V. Day, *A Preaching Workbook* (London: SPCK/Lynx, 1998), p. 111.
2. For a humorous take on this, see the sketch 'The Breakfast Special' by Paul Burbridge and Murray Watts, *Lightning Sketches* (London: Hodder & Stoughton, 1981), p. 183.

1
Richard Bewes

THE ROMANCE OF
OUR LIVES

Richard Bewes was born and brought up in Kenya, as the son of missionary parents. After graduating from Cambridge University, he studied for the Anglican ordained ministry at Ridley Hall, Cambridge. He was to lead the work of parishes in Harold Wood and Northwood, before becoming Rector of the London Church of All Souls, Langham Place – an all-age, multinational congregation that sees some 2,500 people coming through its doors every Sunday. He has long been associated with the work of Dr Billy Graham, having been Chairman of his great 'Mission '89' in London, and is also known for his work with African Enterprise and the Church of England Evangelical Council.

A preacher, broadcaster, and writer of more than 20 books, Richard Bewes' recent titles are Speaking in Public *– Effectively,* The Lamb Wins, The Stone that Became a Mountain, The Top 100 Questions *and* Beginning the Christian Life *(all from Christian Focus).*

Forever I wish to pay tribute to a man called Mr Duxbury. He had been the visiting elocutionist at Ridley Hall theological college in Cambridge, where I did my training for Anglican ordination many years ago. One day it was my turn to have a session with him. Timidly, I came into the room. Mr Duxbury was slightly deaf.

'Right, Mr Bewes,' he began. 'Would you kindly take this Prayer Book and read the opening exhortation for Morning Prayer – as though you were leading the service.'

Gingerly I took the book and started off as impressively as I could:

> Dearly beloved brethren, the Scripture moveth us in sundry places to acknowledge and confess our manifold sins and wickedness; and that we should not dissemble nor cloak them before the face of Almighty God our heavenly Father; but confess them with an …

'Stop!' commanded my guru.

I looked up anxiously.

'What's the matter with you?' enquired Mr Duxbury. 'What's troubling you?'

'Oh … no, nothing. Was I doing it wrong?'

'I was only wondering! Why that funny voice? It sounded so unnatural, so forced. It occurred to me that you'd suddenly had a personality change!'

'Oh, well, no. I was trying to read it with meaning.'

'Meaning, eh? What's the meaning of the word "dissemble", then?'

'Er, well, it means to dispute something, to disagree.'

'It does not. It means to deceive by not saying enough. You'll need to know the meaning of what you're saying, to start with, if you're to have a hope of getting across to a congregation.'

I remained silent. What was coming next?

'Now, Mr Bewes, you're the executive of a company, giving his report to the Annual Meeting. You are about to address the share-holders. Your obvious opening sentence will begin with the words, "Mr Chairman, Ladies and Gentlemen". Think yourself into that meeting. Now, how are you going to say it?'

I took a breath. 'Mr Chairman, Ladies and Gentlemen!'

'Right!' said Mr Duxbury. 'Quite right. Now take up that Prayer Book again. There are people, real people in front of you there. In their own way, they are the shareholders. They have a stake in the church. Start again with that opening exhortation to worship.'

I held the book steady. 'Dearly beloved brethren! The Scripture move…'

BANG! Mr Duxbury had hit the table. I jumped.

'Good, Mr Bewes. Very good. If you can keep that natural approach in your leading and speaking, you'll be a credit to me! Don't want any parsonic voices in the church, do we? Now kindly read aloud for me the greatest story ever told. Here it is, Luke 15. It's a story, remember. Off you go.'

Ridley Hall did many good things for me, but my lesson with Mr Duxbury was the best-spent forty minutes of my two years in that college. I feel deeply indebted to him for saving me from at least some of the pitfalls of public preaching.

Preaching! Let's put our cards on the table straight away. Preaching is the romance of our lives. The whole story for me had begun long before I was born – with my grandpa, Tommy Bewes, in 1882. Tommy was the fourteen-year-old son of a solicitor in Plymouth, the youngest of twelve brothers and sisters. D. L. Moody, the famed American evangelist, was in the middle of a whirlwind tour of Britain, and that week saw him preaching nightly at the Drill Hall in Citadel Road. Tommy went to hear him on Tuesday night, 26 September.

Moody and Sankey: the preacher and the singer. The two celebrities had been criss-crossing throughout the country, becoming a byword in British society, and a butt of music-hall jokes. Now they had reached Plymouth. Tommy wrote on the Friday of that week to his sister Evy. Our family still possesses the letter:

He spoke from the 9th verse of the 3rd of Genesis. It is,

'Where art Thou?' He said that that was the 1st question that God ever asked in the Bible, and that it was the first question that people ought to ask themselves and he said that there were two more that he was going to speak about and they were, 'Where are you going?' and, 'How are you going to spend eternity?' I don't think he could have chosen better ones.

More than three thousand people were packed into the Drill Hall that evening. Who brought Tommy? We think it may have been the parlour-maid, for it is clear that none of the rest of the family attended the meetings. According to the *Western Morning News* next day, 54 people stood at the close of Moody's sermon, to register their decision to follow Christ. Tommy was among them. 'I am glad to see so many young men getting up,' the evangelist was reported to declare. 'They may have forty or fifty years of life before them, and what a great deal they can do for God in that time!'

One sermon: it can be enough to touch and inspire several generations down the line. For Thomas Bewes went on to study at Corpus Christi College at Cambridge University, and from there to Ridley Hall theological college, whose principal was then the famous Handley Moule, later to become Bishop of Durham. Tommy was to serve in the ordained ministry of the Anglican Church, and later helped to found the Rochester Diocesan Evangelical Union. In the event, he was indeed given more than fifty years of active ministry.

His eldest son, Cecil, who was to be my father, also studied at Cambridge, and similarly at Ridley Hall, before ordination and subsequent service with the Church Missionary Society in Kenya. Numbers of Tommy's grandchildren were to enter upon full-time Christian service, and now – a Ridley graduate in my own turn – I am a preaching grandfather myself.

Moody's sermon was only one among hundreds. And Tommy was just one face among thousands! The lesson has never been lost on me. Countless times since I became Rector of All Souls,

Langham Place back in 1983, I found courage from the story of my grandfather. I would clamber into the pulpit, and pray silently: Someone's life is going to be changed by this message from the Bible. Who is it going to be? I may never know. Lord, strengthen my belief that this wonderful thing is going to happen, in the next few minutes.

It is not that we preachers are called upon to plead, Moody-style, for first-time decisions on every occasion. Rather it is that a conviction grows within us that nothing that God has said can be anything other than powerful. God has only to speak a word, and a beautiful blue-green planet comes into existence – glowing with colours, forests and oceans, and teeming with life. That is powerful preaching! Nothing, just nothing, that God has said, can possibly be feeble. If, then, I am proclaiming what God has declared, rather than my own opinions, I ought to be able to expect things to happen, and lives to change – including my own.

How does the call to preach come? Every story is different. For me, it began on the front veranda of our missionary home in Weithaga, on the lower slopes of Mount Kenya, when I was about seven years old. Over the cornflakes we three boys were discussing what we would do when we were grown up. Elizabeth, my sister, had only just been born.

My older brother, Peter, was emphatic. 'I'm going to be a doctor,' he declared. And indeed, in years to come, that very thing happened. Peter was to become a missionary surgeon.

Then my younger brother, Michael, piped up. 'I'm going to be a businessman like Uncle Anstis.' Three decades later the prediction was fulfilled.

But then, on the veranda, all eyes turned on me. 'What are you going to be, Richard?'

I looked down and fidgeted. For the life of me, I couldn't think of anything. Then my mother said something that I was to remember for ever. 'I think that Richard might one day be a church minister.'

The conversation changed. I said nothing, but inwardly my

mother's words settled it. That's it; I'm to be a church minister. And I'm going to preach. Nothing else ever replaced that conviction, not even remotely.

In those heady days of Kenya's burgeoning development, the message of the Bible was steadily taking a hold on great tracts of society. We children were born during the great East African revival that was to sweep many thousands of lives into the churches; where the crowds were sometimes so great on a Sunday that the congregation would have to sit outside church under the trees. Preaching! There was plenty of it. One of its most effective exponents was a Kikuyu lay preacher called Mwangi. People would hang on his every word. Mwangi could tell stories like no one else. He loved the Scriptures and he loved people.

The church elders in Weithaga decided one day to hold a campaign in the area. 'Whom shall we have to lead the mission?' it was asked. One name surfaced above the rest: 'We must have Mwangi.' There was no postal service to speak of, where we lived. People just didn't have letterboxes! We relied on runners. So the call went out verbally, 'Send for Mwangi.'

Nothing happened. No word came back. Mwangi simply couldn't be found. The organisers were getting desperate. Imagine an area-wide campaign that has been proclaimed – and the announced leader has disappeared! Day One of the mission dawned … and suddenly Mwangi turned up.

'Mwangi, at last! Thank God – so you got our message?'

'Message? No. I've heard nothing. Tell me.'

'We've been searching everywhere for you. How is it, then, that you've arrived in Weithaga just in time for the mission?'

'Oh, I've been away in the bush, having a period of prayer and quiet. Then yesterday the Lord said to me, "You're needed in Weithaga." So here I am!'

That's Africa, of course. But all the time the message was penetrating through to me: 'The message of the Bible is powerful, and it is expected to be powerful.'

I was to go to a little boarding school in Nairobi at the age of eight, and then, when I reached thirteen, we all returned as a family to Britain. Later that same year, while we were on a Cornish holiday in Pendeen, I first met the man who, for nearly 22 years would one day be my closest neighbour – a giant among expositors, John Stott. It was he who drove me, in his Jeep, to my first-ever Scripture Union houseparty in Dorset. There I made my teenage decision to be a follower of Jesus Christ. Was this an underlining of things I already knew? For I had never forgotten the 'call' on Weithaga's veranda. All I knew – as I listened to a man called Mr Nash one August evening – was that I had never heard such a wonderful message before; that Christ was standing at the door of my life, and knocking for admission. He had died for the forgiveness of every sin that I had ever committed; he was alive from the dead and he was calling me into personal discipleship and friendship with him for ever! In point of fact I *had* heard the message countless times before, but this time it was definitely targeted at me. I closed with the deal that very night.

Next, it was Billy Graham time! No one will ever understand modern gospel life in Britain today who doesn't understand what happened at London's Harringay Arena over three months in the spring of 1954. Billy Graham, the young 'Hot Gospel' preacher from North Carolina, had come across the Atlantic on the *Queen Mary* and become a national sensation overnight. Within a few weeks he had turned around a hostile press and a cynical public, by the power of his disarming humility and a blazing sincerity. I had left school, but was not yet at university. I went to hear Billy night after night. Sometimes our entire family would attend, bringing friends along with us. One of my tasks was gently to dissuade my deeply devout grandmother, Tommy's widow, from 'going forward'. 'Once she gets down there, we'll never see her again!' was our reasoning.

The crowds were unrelenting, and the mission – initially planned for four weeks – finally ran to sixteen, and ended up filling both the White City and Wembley Stadiums in successive meetings on the same day: 180,000 people. The campaign could have gone on longer. On only four nights in all was Harringay Arena not completely jammed. The message of the meetings was relayed live by Post Office lines to further outlying venues all over the country. Sometimes an extra afternoon matinee meeting had to be improvised. John Stott was then the young Rector of All Souls, and attended every night of the sixteen weeks. Later he was to comment, 'The people were spellbound.' As for myself, it was like a drumbeat in my head: *You are going to be doing this yourself for the rest of your life.* It was a dramatic confirmation of the veranda call, and represented the single most influential three-month period of my life.

The resulting invigoration of Britain's rather struggling 'gospel' constituency – with its backs-to-the-wall mindset – was cyclonic, in virtually every denomination. Here was a vibrant young American preacher, sought out by Churchill, by business tycoons and royalty itself, acceptable in Soho and Windsor Chapel alike, who could mop the floor with the toughest of the Fleet Street cynics – and we loved him. As he gave his nightly call to commitment, future bishops, big-time sports people or small-time gangsters would find themselves standing with hundreds of other enquirers in front of Billy's pulpit and the white wooden railing that surrounded it. I have been bumping into 'Harringay converts' for over fifty years now – in all walks of life.

A few months later I was brought into contact with the mighty evangelist, when – now at Cambridge University – I came onto the small committee that invited him for an eight-day mission among the students. The interest in that mission was worldwide, and hundreds of undergraduates were lastingly touched. Those momentous eight days began for me a friendship with Dr Graham that I have always been honoured to treasure.

I have heard it said many times, 'I could preach a better sermon than Billy Graham.' I am tempted to answer, 'Could you ever take charge of a restless crowd of 60,000 people, quieten it, deal with the hecklers and make Jesus real to the individual tucked away in that seething mass?' For Billy's target was always the individual's heart. When asked by Kenneth Alsop of BBC Television how many 'converts' he was hoping for in a forth-coming campaign, the reply was typical: 'One! Just one. If we can help *one* person towards faith in Jesus Christ, it will have been worth coming across the Atlantic. If I could just win *you* to Christ, it would have been worth the trip!'

Here was a lesson that needs to be relearned again and again. *One in a million.* That was the style of Jesus. Never mind how big the crowd; somewhere in there would be a crooked taxman who needed redemption, a woman with a chronic illness, a parent demented with worry about a dying daughter. Our Lord somehow knew that they were there.

I could recognise this in Dr Graham's approach. As his platform chairman on several occasions in later years, I was captivated by his appeal to the individual, his directness, simplicity and authority; like St Paul, his shunning of the oratorical flourish. In my mind he is right up there with Chrysostom of Constantinople, Bernadino of Siena or Spurgeon of London's East End. For his ability to communicate to vast numbers of people on every continent and for his consistent support for the churches of every hue, Billy Graham has been the most effective evangelist that the Church has been given since the days of the New Testament apostles.

And then there was John Stott. I have learned such a great deal from many wonderfully equipped preachers – but for sheer clarity of exposition, in showing the listener both the meaning and the application of a passage of Scripture, I never heard anyone more effective than 'Uncle John', as he came to be called at All Souls. No wasted words! It would be impossible to edit and shorten the text of a Stott sermon without doing damage to the integrity and unity of the message. The sermons – together with 40 and more books – of this world-travelled expositor have touched scores of countries, and have provided a touchstone of purity and applied scholarship to preachers everywhere.

In one respect, it wasn't too difficult, coming in to lead the work of All Souls' Church for the first time. I never felt threatened by my illustrious forebear. First, I had known him since I was thirteen, and secondly he was so far ahead of us other preachers that we were never remotely in competition.

What was it I learned from those Africans I grew up with? And from the many other compelling preachers whose speaking actually changed lives? A lot of it surely has to do with *conviction*; conviction that what we are about is serious business. As the seventeenth-century Puritan preacher Richard Baxter phrased it: 'I preached, as n'er sure to preach again, and as a dying man to dying men.' Naturally there has to be room for stories and for humour – but in some preachers that I have heard, the whole delivery seems to be an exercise in trying to provide a little padding between the banter and jokes. It is sobering to reflect that of no outstanding preacher was it ever said, 'He was a terribly funny man.'

The other explanation of preaching that has had impact relates to *authority.* If we actually believe that the Book we are holding in our hands is the authoritative and inspired word of God, *it will show in our preaching.* Equally, if we are *not* really convinced about the authority of Scripture, that also will become only too apparent in our entire delivery – the look in the eyes, the tone in the voice, the way we handle the biblical text, in our whole demeanour. It may always be possible that some listeners will be stirred, even riveted by the power of oratory in itself. But no lives will be changed. John Wesley once wrote of a visit to Glasgow: 'I was moved at the sermons I heard, both morning and evening. They contained much truth, but were no more likely to awaken a single soul than an Italian opera.' (*Journals*, 15 May 1774). I have emphasised this point in my book on public speaking. Preaching glows with life-transforming energy when listeners, and some-times the speaker too, are aware that another voice has taken over (*Speaking in Public – Effectively*).

They knew all about this in the New Testament. The apostle Paul puts it vividly when he tells his readers (none of whom had ever seen or heard Jesus): 'But ye have not so learned Christ, if so be that ye have heard him and have been taught by him' (Ephesians 4:20, KJV). It is a pity that modern versions have mistranslated the Greek of this text to read, 'Surely you heard *about* him' – yet the King James Version has it right. The people of Ephesus had only heard preachers, but the apostle says that the person they heard was Jesus! This is the assured outcome of true apostolic proclamation. The preacher fades into the background, and – as at the Transfiguration – we are aware that we are left with Jesus only. 'The Lord was speaking to *me*' is the testimony of thousands of us who, during our lives, have heard the Scriptures being faithfully applied – and, like John Wesley of old, our hearts were 'strangely warmed'.

As for Wesley himself, when you are in Cornwall, pay a pilgrimage to Redruth. Quite near is an impressive hollow in the ground – an old collapsed tin mine, Gwennap Pit. Providing sitting space for thousands, it served as a natural amphitheatre for the preaching of John Wesley – perhaps the greatest man of the eighteenth century, and certainly its most intrepid traveller. The equivalent of ten times round the world on horseback, forty thousand sermons, a journal that became one of the world's long-distance runners in diary output; we tend to wilt at such prodigious feats, and then hear the subtle whisper, *This could never be you*. True, you get a Wesley, a Moody or a Billy Graham only once a century; but we can allow their inspiration to rub off onto us a little!

So, preacher, if you are ever passing through Blackheath in south-east London, pay another pilgrimage to a small clump of scrub, a few yards off the road, right in the middle of the heath. For two centuries and more it has been known as Whitefield's Mount; for indeed, if you step inside this specially preserved part of the original heath, you detect that it comprises a small hillock. There George Whitefield preached, to as many as thirty thousand people. On returning from Africa as a family, our home for ten years was situated 400 yards from this place of Gospel romance, and I would pass it on my way to the Blackheath tennis courts.

There are shrines everywhere for those who know their spiritual history. There is the statue of Eros in London's Piccadilly Circus, with its reminder of the social reformer and missionary statesman Ashley Cooper. Holy Trinity Church in Clapham provided the base from which slave trade abolitionist William

Wilberforce and his friends touched the world. Another Holy Trinity Church – in Cambridge – saw Charles Simeon exercise a nationwide influence during half a century of bitterly opposed preaching. You may visit the Martyrs' Memorial in the centre of Oxford, where Bishops Latimer and Ridley encouraged each other as they perished in the flames ... and you cannot come away unmoved.

Once for my holiday – just for inspiration – I did a pulpit locum in Haworth, Yorkshire, where, generations ago, the sturdy preaching of William Grimshaw gave rise to such a revival in the parish church that no less than 30 bottles of wine would be needed for a single united open-air Communion service. Something had happened to Grimshaw, transforming him from a dejected vicar with no message into a bold spokesman whose ministry lit up the Yorkshire Dales for many miles around. Evidently it had much to do with a rediscovery in Grimshaw's own life of the power of the Scripture message. As one local observer, William Clothier, explained the change in the preaching: 'It was as though God had drawn up Grimshaw's Bible to heaven, and sent him down another!'

The past can be inspiring – but we are not to stay brooding at these shrines. Nostalgia by itself can lead to an unhealthy triumphalism or, alternatively, depression and cynicism. Nor is it productive to wish for the old days to come back – for God never repeats his wonders. For what will he do in our day?

Ever since World War II, the voice of prophecy has moved inexorably in Britain from the church to the theatre. Yet the contention of history – let alone the Scriptures – is that there is nothing like preaching to lift whole groups in a Godward direction. The historian T. R. Glover observed, 'Christianity stabilises society without sterilising it.'

We are to put this to the test. Yes, today. All over again. The Bible is teeming with stories. Tell them! There is a generation around us that has never heard them. There is a power in the Bible all of its own. It only requires *one church*, in every town, village and hamlet in the country, where the pages of the Bible are actually opened and taught, for us to feel a new wind among us – which will be none other than the breath of God himself.

Every day some 100,000 new people are entering into the life of churches across the world. Every week some 1600 new congregations are coming into being that were not in existence the week before. This is a result not so much of brilliant advertising or new church-growth techniques, but more than for any other reason, because there are enough pastors and lay people in country after country around our world who are treating 'the foolishness of preaching' as the romance of their lives. This is a thing that some of us are learning all over again.

2

Mike Breen

LANDMARKS
ALONG THE WAY

Mike Breen (b. 1958) was until recently the Rector of St Thomas' Church, Crookes, Sheffield, the largest Anglican church in the North of England, of which 75 per cent of the members are under thirty-five. He now has an international ministry, working with many different streams and denominations, in addition to being Minister at Large at Community Church of Joy (Lutheran) in Phoenix, Arizona, where he works alongside their team of pastors. He is also an adjunct Professor of Fuller Seminary and began teaching there in 2005. Mike has been preaching, more or less, ever since he became a Christian by himself through reading the Bible at sixteen years old.

Conversion

It was sometime around the age of fifteen that I first became aware of a God consciousness. I had a deep desire to know God. I don't know where it came from; all I can assume now is that it was a sovereign work of God drawing me towards him. Around about that time, it seems as though my brain was rewired to overcome dyslexia. I'd struggled with reading and writing for years and although I had learned to compensate I'd never quite mastered those skills, but suddenly I made enormous strides in my literacy. By the time I was sixteen I was deeply interested in finding out more about God. And after having a conversation with an RE teacher at school, I began to read my Bible at home. The Bible was the first book that I decided to read from cover to cover. Fortunately, this Bible had a reading plan included, so by the time my Old Testament reading got to Numbers, I was able to look at the New Testament and discover for myself the story of Jesus. Pretty much by myself, during the school holiday, I became a follower of Christ, simply by reading the Bible every day.

When I returned to school, I spoke to one of the Christian teachers there. He suggested that I joined a local church and not knowing which one to choose, I joined the one that he went to. It was a church committed to preaching, a church well and truly in the Calvinist tradition. And so I began to hear names like George Whitefield, Spurgeon, Dr Martyn Lloyd-Jones, spoken in hushed tones of respect. I went one evening to the Manchester Free Trade Hall, not far from my home in Cheadle Hulme, and listened to 'the doctor' (Martyn Lloyd-Jones) preach from the text 'Render to Caesar that which is Caesar's, but render to God that which is God's'. I remember being deeply struck by how powerful the preaching was that night. I can remember beginning to lose track of what 'the doctor' was preaching and then suddenly being arrested by his enormous voice booming out the word 'but'. He had given a very clear and detailed exposition of the Christian's civil duties and responsibilities (rendering to Caesar) which, though important, were not particularly exciting to a sixteen-year-old boy. Suddenly the word 'but' rang out through the auditorium. 'But render to God that which is God's.' I saw the fire ignite in his eyes. And the fire in him fell on us all.

As well as this exposure as a 'punter', I also got opportunities early on to find out what it is like to be a 'player'. Val Grieve (a well-known lay preacher in the Manchester area) took me and other young men out with him on preaching engagements and gave us the opportunity to share one point each in the middle of his presentation. I can remember the hard-to-disguise look of disappointment as the congregation were told that these youngsters he had brought along were going to help him preach. I can also remember the fear, as I stood to share the little that I had to offer.

From Oak Hill to ordination (via Hackney)

I was captured by preaching and I was captured by the call to preach. Soon after this I read Lloyd-Jones' book *Preachers and Preaching*. Here I discovered more about George Whitefield – perhaps the greatest of all Calvinist preachers. I soon purchased a secondhand copy of Whitefield's journals and pored over it, so moved by the possibilities of what preaching could achieve. And then at the age of eighteen, I went to Oak Hill Theological College to begin training for the ministry. It was a tender age to begin my training; but it seemed clear that this was God's call and all seemed to attest to the rightness of the decision. I loved Oak Hill and I am deeply indebted to the staff. There I found myself hearing more and more of what it meant to have a biblical ministry and to expound the word of God regularly and rightly to those who would listen.

Rather than going for a selection conference to go forward for ordination at the end of my time in Oak Hill, I felt that I wanted to continue to test my call by working in an inner-city environment, so I went to work with a parish priest called John Pearce in Hackney. I worked with John and his youth worker, Pete Stowe, and there began to realise that for all my training, expository preaching was never going to be enough to engage with the disenfranchised young people of Hackney who knew little of the Bible and understood even less of the rational processes needed to follow a well-argued sermon.

As more young people in the area began to follow Christ, we started the 'Teen Service', which met every Sunday night in the youth club. There I discovered a gift for telling stories and also the effect of storytelling on people who had little grasp of the Bible story themselves. I told the story of Jesus and I serialised *The Pilgrim's Progress* and other Christian classics. These quickly became the centrepiece of the teen service. I can remember the groan that would go up as I left yet another cliff-hanger for next week: 'Christian is facing Appollyon the dragon, about to be con-sumed … and we'll find out next week what happened.' 'No, tell us what happened now!' I was beginning to learn how to carry the listeners with a story, which I furnished with exegetical insights and expository thoughts, to illustrate what I was trying to convey.

Later, as a curate in a parish church in Cambridge – in 'the town' rather than 'the gown' area – my opportunities grew. I was given the responsibility of the youth and community centre called Romsey Mill and here again I was challenged to find a way of communicating the Gospel in a method that young people could understand. We used dance music, drama, parables and storytelling all tied together in what we called 'The Romsey Mill Roadshow'. We would use contemporary music to highlight the questions that so often were in the minds of young people, drama and storytelling to explore those questions, and simple direct 'Gospel bullets' to call the youngsters to a response. This, like many other experiences of seeking to engage with a culture unfamiliar with Christian teaching, continued to fashion my understanding of what it is to preach.

From Brixton to Sheffield and Generation X

After Cambridge, with my wife and family, I moved to Brixton. And there we discovered cultural challenge in a way that we had not encountered before. Brixton was a melting pot that in many ways was a forerunner to society today. It was as though Brixton (like other inner-city communities in Western countries) was experiencing early what all of us have come to recognise as normal. It felt like chaos. In the midst of this chaos people were asking questions, and their questions needed to be taken seriously. There in that church in Brixton both I and the team that had joined us sought to engage with the problems of communicating the Gospel to a culture and community in freefall. Again, we used drama and visuals and dance – whatever we could take hold of to give us a chance to express what we knew to be life-changing answers. Most of all, we wanted to offer a life-changing encounter with God. This encounter most often happened in corporate worship and as God's Word was preached.

The age group that I've worked with most has, of course, grown older as I've moved on in ministry. To begin with, I taught children at a Sunday school in Cheadle Hulme, then teenagers in Hackney. By the time I got to Sheffield, at St Thomas's Church, this generation had become young adults. They are called Generation X. Here in Sheffield we've seen many of this generation come to Christ and choose to follow him in a radically committed way. And preaching is central to the experience of God impacting this generation as we come together corporately. What I've discovered as I've followed the narrative of God's leading in my life is that we need to learn to read the Scriptures *and* read people's culture so that we can share the Gospel. Often by circuitous routes I have found that God has trained me in cross-cultural communication. Charles Spurgeon said more than a hundred years ago that a good preacher had the Bible in one hand and the newspaper in the other. Perhaps today it's a Bible in one hand and a remote control in the other (or maybe even a computer mouse).

Acts 17: Paul in Athens

Effective communication of the Gospel is not a new task, and effective preaching is most certainly not a new phenomenon. When I think of the apostle Paul in Athens, struggling to communicate the Gospel to the people of that city, I find myself instructed and illuminated, but the principles he seems to follow help me with the missionary task of reaching the group to which I've been sent.

When Paul arrived in Greece at the harbour city of Piraeus, he saw the immediate and obvious articulation of a great culture – the artefacts, the ceramic works, the enormous sculptures and sacred temples that lined the road to the great western gate of Athens. He was struck by the fact that for every occasion gods were worshipped. So there was a god that covered every hope and aspiration for each season of life – children, marriage, work, future, past, education, friends, even enemies. There were gods for every conceivable circumstance. And because some circumstances could not be predicted, and also because the people assumed that not all of the gods had been revealed to them, they even made altars to unknown gods.

Paul's response: 'The Five Card Trick'

Preaching to educated people is something that the churches in Britain have done for a long time, and the Church of England in particular has made a specialism of it. We have focused on the intelligentsia and the social élite for much of our history (I believe that it's a mistaken strategy, but nevertheless that's what we've done). Consequently, the cultured Anglican sermon has been the epitome of how to preach in church to educated audiences.

The basic method is 'The Five Card Trick', consisting very simply of an introduction, three points and a conclusion. That's the way that I was taught at theological college and it's an easy and understandable way to communicate important information. It's interesting to note that, years earlier, Paul did exactly the same thing. He used an introduction to get a hearing from his audience by making them feel comfortable and getting them on his side. He then presented his three points. He said that God made all things, that God made humanity from one person and we can find that person in creation. God is very near, he said, and we must put our trust in him, rather than in things made of wood or stone. He concluded by explaining that God will judge according to our response to him, and the judge will be a man God has raised from the dead.

Is there a similar process of cultural observation leading to effective communication that we can use today? This question has always been in the background as I have attempted to preach. Television, the internet, mobile phones, music and film: today our cultural artefacts are saying something to the careful observer. I believe this is a fundamental skill that the Lord wants to teach us – to look deeply, to see beyond the surface, so that we can say something of significance. As we read Scripture we need also to learn to 'read' our culture. Let me share how I use these observations to help inform my proclamation of the Gospel. Following Paul's example of culturally sensitive communication, let me suggest my 'Five Card Trick'.

Card 1

I use anything – the last film I watched, TV, music, the news. I have observed that just below the surface, most people have deep questions waiting to emerge, questions that presuppose the existence of God and a need for him to intervene. I believe that society's communication with itself through the arts reveals what these questions are and offers a way in. I observe the artefacts of our culture, keeping my eyes and ears open and looking for the opportunity that some circumstance may afford. But my intro-duction needs to touch on this universally held belief that the world is in trouble and 'out of control' and the solution is beyond our ability to find. I believe that the most important word I can share, the revelation for our culture, is this: 'God loves you.'

I aim to speak to people's hearts and tell them that God can heal. We regularly pray for healing in our Sunday services at St Thomas, and also at our regular times of prayer during the week. Church members and others who have no connection with church attend, believing that God can heal. People need to know that God loves us and so wants to heal, transform and meet us; not just that he can, but that he wants to. It's important to tell people that God is in the world, loves the world, can change the world and wants to – starting with them.

Card 2

Secondly, I try to help people understand that there is a cosmic war happening right now. God has an enemy who does not want God to have a relationship with us or any other part of his creation. God's enemy has usurped control over creation, so there is going to be a fight for freedom and love. But we can win this because the decisive battle has been won. I emphasise that God is calling us into a relationship with him, but that relationship with God has been ruined by the enemy of our souls. The enemy has exploited our self-indulgence and our self-centredness and has snatched away our chance to be with God and to know the good things that God wants to pour out on us.

I believe that it is very important for the preacher to ask questions of his listeners and so I ask them: 'When you look at the world, do you think, how can it ever change? When you hear of wars, when you hear about the ecological disaster standing on the very doorstep of our lives, the inner cities, the poor, the brutalised, do you wonder what we can do?'

I think it is highly important to address how people these days try to cope with their fears and anxieties. I also think it is important to be direct and honest and realistic about the different methods that young people today use to deaden their pain.

What do you say to people like that? Well, you say: 'The world has an enemy. You know it when you try to abate the fears in your heart, there's an enemy out there, unseen and unnamed, and you feel that this enemy is out to get you. Sometimes we give the enemy a name. We call it cancer, AIDS or international terrorism. This lack of peace in our hearts is still there, and when we switch the light off at night we still feel afraid. The world's been ruined, it's been twisted, by an enemy and the blessings have been blighted.'

I find that if I look carefully at the products of contemporary culture – films, music, artefacts – I see that this is what the world is saying to us, this is what society is trying to communicate to us. I believe we need to recognise these things, identify with them and stand with those we are seeking to reach so that the good news meets and overcomes the bad news.

Sometimes I will say: 'I've not been able to fix the problem myself, I've not been able to quiet the fears in my own heart, I've not been able to take away the anxiety, but what I've discovered is this: God has sent someone and he has given me peace. I've met a person who in the midst of my sense of hopelessness and my sense of powerlessness has given me peace and power. He's given me peace every day to live, every day to sleep. He's given me peace about tomorrow, about my family and my relationships. He's given me a peace that cannot be removed because it's peace within my heart, not peace that's created by circumstance. It's not peace of the moment, the beautiful sunset or the great feeling, or the emotional high, it's something within. It's a gift and he's given it to me and it never goes away. Even when I am afraid I still have this peace, the peace of God. The person who gave me this peace fought for it and won it for me. His name is Jesus.'

Card 3

Most important of all in my sermon is the message that a decisive battle has been won against our enemy and that we have power. Not only do we have the antidote to the anxiety, but also now we have a weapon to use against the enemy who continues to seek to rob us and others of this relationship. The power is this: God's presence in our hearts brings us peace, a peace that beats with the rhythm of good news. This news tells us that there is a future world that God is making. This is so important to impart because it brings a message of hope: although there is a strong enemy, we have one on our side who is stronger and as long as we choose not to give up, we will certainly win. I always bring in the resurrection here.

Card 4

My next 'card' is to ask people to respond and to embrace God's solution (salvation/rescue), to participate in what he has to offer. I call my audience to 'embrace the solution. Embrace the peace and power that comes from the presence of God.' I have come to understand that people today are not as conscious of sin as they are of their own anxiety and I have adapted my preaching accordingly. That's just the reality. The Gospel is the same: we are forgiven! We have been restored to a relationship with God. But we have got to start where people are, not where *we* are. People are where anxiety is – *not* where guilt is. Now, there's a lot of guilt around and there's a lot of anxiety about guilt. But the principal experience that people want to deal with is anxiety or fear.

Card 5

Last of all I believe I have to introduce to my audience the idea that there is an alternative and to excite them with the idea that they can join the community of the opposition and change the world. The introduction was: 'the world is out of control'. But the conclusion is this: 'you can change the world'. It can be changed by a new community of revolutionaries committed to living in the presence of God and bringing the benefits of this life to others. That's a very different conclusion from the introduction. And it's the kind of conclusion that gives hope to a hopeless world.

How I try to communicate the message

So that is the content and construction of a 'Gospel' I regularly seek to share with others, a Gospel that has produced profound effects in the context of post-modern young people. But as well as content, construction and context, there is *communication*, and specifically the method of communication. As I said earlier, I have discovered story as the principle method of conveying the message. This is not to say that every sermon is a story from beginning to end – rarely so, in fact – but it means that story-telling constitutes a central part of the communication process. To develop as a preacher, I've sought to improve my skill by listening to good storytellers.

This began with my parents and members of my extended

family, where the storytelling culture of northern England was still very much alive. This culture developed around the hearth and in the home of many working-class families. I can remember finding on old reel-to-reel Phillips tape recorder in my parents' attic. When I finally got the old tapes to work, I discovered that most of them were records of my grandfather and others telling stories from their lives. It was amazing to me at the time to think that somebody had gone to so much trouble to record these stories.

In more recent years, I've looked around for models of story-telling and have discovered stand-up comedians! First, Billy Connolly, then others like Eddie Izzard and Peter Kay have profoundly informed me in the art of storytelling. Basically these incredibly gifted comedians make observations from their own and others' lives and convey the humour they find through the telling of a story.

Sometimes, to be provocative, when people ask me who are my greatest influences as a preacher, I'll name one of these comedians and smile at the shock on their faces! Of course, I then go on to explain that these are the best examples I can find of the folk art of storytelling still present within our culture. My own view is that the growth in popularity of these stand-up comedians is largely due to that lack of a connecting story, the lack of a meta-narrative, which we looked at earlier.

A final word from the heart of a preacher

> When I came to you, brothers, I did not come with elo-quence or superior wisdom as I proclaimed to you the testimony about God. For I resolved to know nothing while I was with you except Jesus Christ and him crucified. I came to you in weakness and fear and with much trembling. My message and my preaching were not with wise and persuasive words but with a demonstration of the Spirit's power, so that your faith might not rest on men's wisdom, but on God's power. (1 Corinthians 2:1–5)

Paul said he came 'in weakness'. For all his learning and insight Paul chose not to present himself but another – 'Jesus Christ – and him crucified'. For me, the same process of brokenness and weakness experienced by Paul as a context for God's power has been an ever-present reality.

The way that this has been brought home to me over the years is by God revealing to me that even though I do have some gifts, I am the recipient of God's grace, and there are huge areas of brokenness in my life. In previous years, if left to my own devices, I would have worked too hard and ignored the people closest to me. The reason I did this is because I genuinely believed that by working harder I could make a greater difference. Now that does occur in the short term, but if we take that on as a habit and then as a lifestyle, what we are saying to God is that we are responsible for our own lives and we are going to bring change by our own effort and not by his grace. Eventually we begin to strive so much that we become the god of our own lives. I did that – and God brought me to the point of burn-out. It seemed as though he was saying, 'OK, just keep on working in your own strength and we will see if it brings you the break-through you are looking for.' Of course it didn't. The only breakthrough it produced was in me. Once it had occurred, the Lord has had me revisit my weakness – my fundamental need of him – several times. In just about every place where I've been called to preach and lead, God has allowed my weakness to be exposed. This is something which I can now much more embrace, as I see the effects in my life. As I recognise my need God seems to step in.

I have discovered a great truth as a preacher: our lives are broken, like the pieces of a broken pot. Mine too. Whether we know it or not, we are a broken people. From time to time, we will become aware of our brokenness. There are options, I've discovered: we can give up, just keep trying, or recognise the brokenness and put it into the hands of God. As I put my broken-ness into God's hands, he's able to hold broken pieces together because his hands are bigger than mine. In time, I've seen more broken pieces in my life and instead of trying to fix them, hide them or do something with them, I put these pieces into his hands as well. The cracks are still there, but I am held together. Brokenness in the hands of God becomes wholeness. Weakness in the hands of God becomes strength. Foolishness in the hands of God becomes wisdom.

As he died on the cross, Jesus said, 'Father into your hands I commit my spirit'. In dying, Jesus gave testimony to the way he lived every day: he placed his life into the hands of his Father and let his Father hold his life together and on course. His Father was glorified, and free to release unlimited power upon him. That's what I want to learn as I seek to follow Jesus, as a preacher, as a man.

There's an old fable from the Indian subcontinent of a poor water carrier. He would earn just a small amount every day for carrying water for a rich man. He carried the water in two vases on the end of a large stick held across his shoulders. One vase was complete and the other was cracked. The complete vase would belittle the cracked vase and say, 'I'm a lot better than you. I can carry more water than you. I'm much more useful to our master, because I can carry more water than you.' And the broken vase was belittled and silenced by the mockery. But as the water carrier walked from the well to the fine house, the broken vase would leave a trail of water on every journey. In that trail of water seeds began to grow. When people walked on the path they commented on how beautiful the flowers were on one side of the path. The brokenness of one vase was used as a blessing for others.

Weak, broken people make the best preachers because preaching is foolishness. 'But God chose the foolish things of the world to shame the wise; God chose the weak things of the world to shame the strong.' (1 Corinthians 1:27) To engage in such a foolish activity in the hope of communicating a life-changing message, you've got to be weak (or perhaps certifiable). Here the mystery of preaching is found – a foolish activity that requires weakness and exposes brokenness in the preacher. But in these apparent deficiencies the all-sufficiency of Jesus and his Gospel is revealed.

We need to understand that as others sit to listen, we stand not simply to speak, but like a servant at a table, to serve, giving to those who are seated what has been prepared for them as a meal. Sometimes the meal is simple; sometimes it includes special delicacies that have taken a long time to prepare. As we think of ourselves as preachers, we ought not to think of ourselves as great influencers – more as weak people in the hands of a strong God; weak people with an astonishingly powerful message – the message of the cross – to communicate. I believe that this perspective liberates preaching. It liberates us from performance. It liberates us from seeking the approval of our listeners. It liberates us from attempting to be clever, or appearing to be intelligent. As Paul says, 'Where is the wisdom of the wise or the intelligence of the intelligent?' All these things appear to be little or nothing in the face of God's great wisdom, and Jesus Christ crucified, which we proclaim in our preaching.

These have been the touchstones, the foundations, on which I have sought to develop and grow in my calling to preach. And I believe that they are the orientation by which I want to continue to follow this calling.

3
Steve Chalke

COMMUNICATING
THROUGH STORY

Steve Chalke was ordained as a Baptist minister in 1981, having studied at Spurgeon's Theological College in London, and was a local minister for four years before setting up the Oasis Trust in order to open a hostel for homeless young people. Steve has presented his own television series for ITV and BBC, as well as a regular show on Radio 4. He was awarded an MBE in the New Year's Honours List 2004 for his services to social inclusion. Steve is forty-nine years old and is married to Cornelia.

In this chapter, based on an interview conducted in June 2004, he tells of his call to preach, early influences, his belief in story and illustrations, and his passion for communication.

How did you receive your call to preach?

When I was fourteen I started going to a church called Holmesdale Baptist Church in South Norwood. I guess they must have had epilogues and things like that after the table tennis, but I can't really remember. But what I do remember is this: one Friday night I was walking home up Dixon Road in

South Norwood and I thought to myself: if this is true, that God loves me, that Christ gave his life for me, then I'm going to spend the rest of my life telling people that this is true. It's either true or it's not, and if it's not true then what am I messing about in this youth club for, even if Mary Hooper is fanciable? But if it is true, I'm going to spend the rest of my life telling people about Jesus and when I grow up I'm going to set up a hostel, a hospital and a school for the poor. I got home and my mum said, 'Have you had a nice evening?' and I said, 'Yes, I think I've become a Christian, and I'm going to spend the rest of my life telling people about Jesus and when I grow up I'm going to set up a hostel, hospital and school for the poor.' And she said – my dad was away doing shift work – she said, 'Very nice.' And that is the story of my life, really, that evening, because everything I've been involved in since, the whole of Oasis, everything I do is a response to that night.

Who gave you your models for preaching?

When I was a kid I'd gone to that same Baptist church, so I'd grown up going to lots and lots of services and, in fact, three on Sunday: morning, afternoon Sunday school and then evening. I'd got bored – because it's very boring – and so I kind of pulled out of that and then went back to the youth club. Running this youth club were a bunch of students from Spurgeon's College, because the church was just down the road from the college. I can't remember anything that was said but I was inspired by them as people. I remember Graham Kendrick came in. He was a student at Goldsmiths College and he came and sat on a stool and played the guitar and I was inspired by all of these people and the fact that they had something to say about their faith. I suppose I wanted to be like that.

Then, what led me on was a guy called Steve Flashman. Steve was one of these guys at Spurgeon's College. I was fourteen, he must have been twenty-two or twenty-three and he set up a band called Manna, with his wife and himself, his nephew, Keith

Loring, and me. So every Saturday we'd go off and do these evangelistic concerts in youth clubs and halls around the country in an old GPO van painted yellow that Steve had. Steve is a brilliant communicator and always did the evangelistic talk at the end. I remember we were driving off to this gig and he said, 'Why don't you do it tonight?' When you're fourteen or fifteen or sixteen you think, 'Of course, he's asked me to do it because he's an old man. I'm young, I understand. He's old, he understands that.' And I still remember some of the things I said. I remember a talk that I gave on the Isle of Sheppey, Sheerness, and recall how horrendous it was, and on the way back Steve saying, 'You know, when you said they're all sinners and going to hell, do you really think that was the most positive start?' Of course I'd defend it, and he never put me down and so I grew as a communicator in that way. I would say Steve, first of all, because he believed in me when nobody should have done.

After I'd finished my A Levels at school (which I failed, by the way), I then worked with him for a year in Ashford where he was by then the minister and he allowed me to be the youth leader. That was at the age of eighteen, and I got to speak every week and he gave me the opportunity to speak sometimes in the church services.

Then when I was twenty-one I met a guy called David Beer. David's a good communicator, and has been a fantastic friend to me through the years. I worked with him for a year before going to Spurgeon's College and then afterwards I went to work in Tonbridge in Kent for four years with him. Again, I was given lots of opportunity and experience. So I have always worked with people who have given me the opportunity, which has been fantastic.

The most inspirational character and good friend to me has been Tony Campolo. He's been a great mentor to me. By then, time had moved on and I was being asked to speak at this place and that. I often found myself in countries where I didn't really know what I was doing or why I was there, and Tony was often there, because he was asked to speak at these things too. He's had a fantastic, empowering effect on my life because he's given me time and I've been able to sit and listen as well as have his friendship and encouragement.

How long have you been using story in your preaching?

I remember when I was at Spurgeon's College I was asked to go and speak at the Crusaders' seventy-fifth anniversary in the Royal Festival Hall. Because it was such a big thing in our terms, back at Spurgeon's the year above me gave me a bit of a grilling. I remember some people saying, 'Well, you can only communicate in stories and you can only communicate to young people' and at that point – you know you're challenged.

We had this thing called Sermon Class that we used to have to go and endure – either endure being the one who was preaching the sermon or endure the sermons that were being preached, and a lot of them were pretty boring. I learned through that whole experience. Both times I had to preach I told stories and people laughed and it went down well. I was criticised exegetically, but I remember thinking, 'No. Stories work.'

People enjoy stories. I spoke just this morning and I told some stories. If you tell stories to kids of seven and old people of eighty, you've got to hold everyone's attention all at the same time. It's not easy to do unless you use stories, but once you use stories, it is. And you can say profound things through a story that's simple, if you learn the art. I told a story this morning; it was a picture really; I just said, 'You know, the tree needs the soil and without the soil it will die. The soil needs the rain and without the rain it will die. The rain needs the cloud – no cloud, no rain – the cloud needs the air and the air needs the tree. There's a circle of life – we link to one another and when we forget that we're all lost.' The kids get it and the grandparents get it. If you learn to tell stories well you don't even have to apply them afterwards. That's the great thing, because you can actually say that the tree needs the soil and the soil needs the rain and the rain needs the cloud and the cloud needs the air and the air needs the tree. It's like that for you and me. And you can stop. In fact, it's better if you do stop. So stories, yes, are it. And Jesus did that – told stories, asked questions, told stories, asked questions, and that's all he did, 90 per cent of what he did.

Who are the communicators who have made the strongest impact on you?

I've always been influenced by people who I believe can speak simply. I would say this (in fact, I think C. S. Lewis said this, in essence): 'He who understands deeply will communicate simply. He who doesn't understand will be forced to use long words.'

One of the best things that ever happened to me was the day when through the work of Oasis, about 15 years ago now, I got the opportunity to make radio and television programmes, and through this I got involved in the world of politics. Those two worlds, the political world and the media world, have been a fantastic balance for me to the church world in which I operate. I have learned through having to think through my faith in ways that I can explain to a television audience or a radio audience or in a debate programme, and through having to talk about my faith clearly. You don't have the chance to come out with your smart theological answer. The question always comes at you slightly sideways. So although you've got an answer prepared and you've got your theological thing all sorted and you know what the Bible says about abortion or whatever, the question comes in sideways and you can't use the smart answer, the prepared answer. That forces you to think, rather than 'Ah, there's the question, here's the standard answer'; it forces you to think. That's been a very good discipline for me over the years.

Can you tell me something about your speaking technique?

The reason most preachers don't work on TV is because they

preach and television is about something altogether different. It's not about the crowds, it's about fireside chat, a talk with a friend. So I always say to people, love the camera – I was taught that – make the camera your friend. You're sat there over a glass of wine with your friend, and the friend is the camera. So you chat, you talk like this, whereas the preacher wants to … (loud voice) and it's all in your face. I've seen it happen many times when I've tried to interview preachers for television and radio. They want to get across their three points instead of having a conversation and see where it goes. I think that has helped me a lot with my style of delivery.

This morning, I talked to a hugely non-church audience – a couple of hundred – and actually what I'm doing is just chatting to them, I'm not preaching. I start off by having a chat with them.

I have studied (though never professionally) the other bits of this: movement and presentation skills. I say to people constantly that our words are not our major communication vehicle. Public speakers and communicators fall into the trap of thinking that their voice is the major tool. I know it's natural, and we talk about voice before we talk about everything else, but actually the way it works is entirely the other way round. It's to do with movement, with eye contact; it's to do with smile, it's to do with gestures and using your hands and moving towards an audience, not standing back from them, and not looking down, and letting your voice rise and fall.

When I'm nervous – and I'm always nervous when I'm doing something I've not done before – I deliberately practise my first line so I don't stand up and say, 'Oh, ah, er…' And I'll purposely make myself do the things that I know I would do if I was relaxed, so I'll stand on a stage and push myself to step forward and I'll push myself to use my hands and I'll push myself to smile, even though it feels unnatural to me.

You know that experience, when you stand up and tell a story and you get to the end and no one even cracks their frown – there's not a titter? It's a common experience for a communicator, a preacher. Because they are unsure, they build in their best illustration or the funniest joke at the front, in order to get the audience or the congregation on their side. They deliver it and no one smiles, which they read as, 'This really isn't working. They're not on my side.' This makes the person more nervous and then it's a downward spiral. What I learned was, it's nothing to do with them not finding me funny. It's to do with body movement. When I stand up, I'm nervous. Through my body movements and through the look on my face and the use of my voice, the audience or congregation can smell my nervousness and they see it. This is all a subconscious thing for them as well as me. They sense my insecurity and nervousness and therefore they are nervous for me. They are not against me. I've seen it happen to so many other people standing on stage. Because I'm thinking either consciously or subconsciously, 'He's nervous', when he cracks a joke I'm not going to laugh because I'm as nervous as he is. I'll only laugh when I'm relaxed and I'll only be relaxed if I think the communicator is relaxed. So it's the communicator's job to learn to give off that sense of being relaxed even if he or she is as nervous as they come.

So is it simply a skill you can learn?

I think that communication is a gift. The principal is simply this: Charles Spurgeon, a great preacher, said, 'If someone can preach, I can train him to do better. If a man can't preach, there's nothing I can do.' I could train forever to be a ballet dancer and I'm not going to get very far, so I do think if you have a basic skill, it can be improved. But it's a lot of hard work and you've got to keep working at it.

I enjoy speaking. Because Oasis is as it is, I can get very bogged down in office work. I can deal with it so long as I get some oxygen – for me, that is to stand up and communicate and I don't mind whether that's to a crowd or through a microphone or through a camera. I'm not fussed about the context. I enjoy writing as well. I do a lot of writing, but I feel that the thing I enjoy doing most in life is communicating ideas.

Tony Campolo has been really helpful to my motivation as well. We were in Harare in nineteen-eighty-something, at the Sheraton Hotel. It was the Baptist World Youth Alliance Conference and it was packed, it was huge. I think there were four or five thousand people from around the world. I sat and talked to Tony, and he said, 'How do you feel?'

I said, 'Tony, I just don't think I should speak because it's all about me. I'm going to stand up and I'm just so arrogant about all of this. I think they will all look at me and think Steve Chalke's a good speaker, or he's not a good speaker, or whatever, and my motive has become to impress them all and I'm just worried about that. I can't do it.'

Tony sat there and put his hand on my knee and said, 'Steve, let me tell you something. We haven't really got time to work out your motives. That's going to take us an awful long time. Why don't you get on and do it? When you retire, perhaps we can have a little session about what it is that motivated you.' (Laughter.) And it was a fantastic piece of advice which I've given to loads of people since. The point is, God's Kingdom is a lot more important than our little motives. Let's get on and deliver, and sort it all out afterwards.

How do you feel after you've preached?

The other thing I've learned about communication, through the years, is that you never know how well or badly you've done. I learned that early on. Sometimes I would feel like I was going down like a lead balloon, when you can't get a smile on anyone's face and you seem to be communicating with absolutely no one, but you're stunned by the take-up and the response over the next few days, the next few weeks, or even months or years. Just incredible. People would come up to me, as I'm sure as they do to any communicator, and say, 'What you said then was fantastic!' Do you know, so many times I thought that can't be true, but it is. Then other times I will think I've made a point very well and it seems to make absolutely no impact on anyone. So the speaker's view of what he or she is saying is far too subjective to be capable of measurement. So you've just got to get out there, do it, and give it your best shot. You constantly learn.

Also, you never feel as if you've done a great job. Every time you drive home or sit in a corner with a cup of coffee after you've spoken, you are always analysing. I'm thinking if only I could have done this, and if I'd have done it …

Leading on from that, people sometimes say to me, 'Oh, doesn't it get boring or wooden if you use the same talk again?' Actually Charles Spurgeon said, 'A talk's not worth listening to until you've preached it fifty times' or something like that. But it's true, it comes to life. One of the greatest things I've learned from redaction criticism is this: Jesus did not have very many talks. (Laughter.) That seems to me to be the greatest thing from the redaction critics. Jesus had only a handful of talks and he kept giving them. He loved repeating himself.

How do preachers learn to preach at your church here?

Here, almost every Sunday now we have something called the Sunday Debate or something called Grill the Preacher. Basically, the rule is the preacher can preach for 15 minutes (or less), then the debate begins and can last as long as he's spoken for. Anyone can ask the preacher anything about what was said, and challenge anything. We have fantastic debates. It does two things. It involves everyone and it's just amazing the people who start talking. We've got all sorts of people, young lawyers to little old ladies in their eighties or pensioners who have never moved past the Lambeth Walk, as Cockney as they come, and they all jump in and start. We do it like a Kilroy thing. We do that and we get fantastic debates going on, everybody chatting and talking. Someone was saying to me yesterday, the biggest difference about this church from any other one they've ever been to is that the preacher definitely isn't on a pedestal or in a pulpit, but everything's challengeable. So it does something for the

congregation because everyone's learning from one another and
not just from what *you* say. The other thing, it doesn't half make
the preacher think. There's no point standing up here and saying
stuff that you are not sure of because someone would rip through
it (though nicely). That Sunday Debate or Grill the Preacher is
really interactive.

How do you keep in touch with the concerns of your listeners?

You can tell how relevant a Christian preacher is to their culture
by taking a ride with them in their car. You look at their stack of
CDs or tapes and the more worship and ministry tapes they've
got, the more disconnected they will be. Their understanding of
their culture is related inversely to the size of their ministry tape
stack. So I say to them, take your ministry tapes and worship
CDs out, and turn that radio on. The only time I ever really listen
to the news or to music or know what's happening, is in the car.
You can listen to Radio 4 and catch what's going on and serious
debate. You can turn on Radio 1 and listen to that culture. Here
in London you listen to Melody or Capital or Heart FM or
whatever. So you are listening to your culture. A diet of Radio 4
will make you as cynical and as arrogant as some of the
presenters appear. A diet of London Capital Radio and Heart will
make you as shallow as they seem to be, so it's about mixing it
up and listening. I suppose at the end it doesn't matter how you
get your news intake as long as you are getting lots of news
intake and debate as well. So, for me, a programme on BBC1 like
Question Time is great. I know that's out on the cerebral end of
things, but it's about debate. Someone says something and you
think, 'Oh, that's a good point' and then someone else says, 'Oh
no, that's wrong,' and they give you the other point and you
think, 'Oh, that's a good point', and then someone else, etc. Then
you think, 'They can't all be good points! I agreed with them all,
but they conflict.' So it forces you to think. I believe that's hugely
important for preaching.

Do you see yourself as an expository preacher?

On a serious level on the whole issue of exegesis, and I'm not knocking him at all, but Martin Lloyd-Jones, for instance, would be held up to be a great expositor of the Bible. At Spurgeon's we'd all got endless racks of Martin Lloyd-Jones' books. I would say of him it wasn't exegesis, it was what I would call now eisegesis. It's reading *into* the text, not reading *out of* the text. So he gets to Ephesians and there's this phrase 'But God ...' and people say he preached for six weeks on 'But God'. Great. It's like one of those coat-hangers over there. Here's a coat-hanger, now what can I chuck on that?

If we really grapple with the text, in its context and its culture, we have such powerful things to say to our society. For example, Genesis Chapter 1. What this passage means today is not the primary question, it's the secondary question. The primary question is: what did this passage mean in its original context to its original hearers? What did the man or woman who first wrote this mean? How was it understood? So you've got to contextualise before you can recontextualise. There's no dispute amongst the scholars that Genesis 1 was written in Babylon in the Exile. Psalm 137: 'By the rivers of Babylon, we sang and wept and mourned...' In Babylon, the people of Israel asked the question, 'How can we sing the Lord's song in this strange land? How can we articulate it?' And one of the ways they do that is to write Genesis Chapter 1. It says that God who is good created the earth. Male and female, he created them both and he said, 'It's good.'

The Babylonian creation story or myth is about the gods' vengeance and violence and sexual abuse and man subjugating woman. Of course, every story is written to teach values of some sort, and this warrior race, the Babylonians, had a creation story which legitimised their lifestyle, which was to be a warrior people who abused women. The Babylonian creation story tells us that vengeful gods, who hate one another and war on one another, create the universe. If you look out at the stars, it's the corpse of the mother god, and so in the Babylonian creation story, creation is out of violence and it's out of the abuse of women. The writers of Genesis 1 sit down and they say, 'In the beginning there was a God who created the heavens and the earth out of love and he looked at it all, male and female he created them, and he said it is good.' Fantastic. Now that is something worth telling our culture about. And that's what I mean about real exegesis and that you have to understand deeply to explain simply.

The funny thing is, I could take what we've just said and I could sit with some of these people who live on this estate and I could tell them that story and they would be motivated by it. There is a God behind the universe who cares about me. If you argue about six-day creation with them, they'll think you are completely barking mad!

4

Ian Coffey

PREACHING WITH
PASSION

Ian Coffey is a Baptist minister and currently Senior Pastor of Crossroads International Church, Geneva and member of the Spring Harvest Leadership Team. Ordained in 1975, he has led churches in Essex and Devon and preached in many parts of the world.

A picture, an anecdote and an important point

Let me begin with the picture.

A winter Sunday morning, 1961, Kingston upon Thames, Surrey.

The church building is large and framed in mahogany-stained wood. The ceiling is high and supported by solid oak trusses. The pews are ranked in rigid rows all facing forward to the pulpit that looks like the prow of an old sailing vessel. It stands between heaven and earth and offers the preacher a lofty view across the scattered congregation. There are few children among them. Many are elderly, while all are well dressed. Neat, scrubbed and Sunday-bested from top to toe, they are listening hard to the earnest urgings of the preacher who stands shrouded in a black robe that hides a black suit. One piece of relief is allowed – the twin white tabs that protrude at the neck, offering the merest glimpse of light in the dark canopy. The preacher is animated in his pleas as his arms move up and down and his body turns, his head dipping and rising with the changes in tone of his voice.

Look carefully to the right – midway down the church, under the balcony and you will spot the subject. A boy of about ten years of age, pudding-basin haircut and clad in a suit that looks a size small. Suits usually have a jacket, sometimes a waistcoat, and trousers – long trousers. But not our subject. His are short trousers that look both tiny and tight. The ensemble looks ridiculous but the boy seems unconcerned. Watch him carefully as he fidgets alongside a middle-aged woman who is his mother. He seems oblivious to whatever the rest find riveting and divides his time between drawing and writing on scraps of paper and peering around the Victorian building, scanning every detail of its patterned glass and chiselled tablets. Occasionally he leans into the protective arm of his mother, resting his head against her and trying to sleep.

Next the anecdote.

Harold Macmillan was British Prime Minister from 1957–63. His wife has been described as a reluctant political wife although she dutifully accompanied her husband to a plethora of events. Once, when he was giving a speech in Halifax, a heckler in the crowd shouted, 'Does the speaker know his wife is asleep?'

Lady Macmillan woke and replied, 'My father's a politician, my brother's a politician, my husband's a politician, my son's a politician and my son-in-law's a politician. I've heard it all before. So if you don't mind, I'm going back to sleep.'

And the point?

Quite a lot can happen when you appear to be asleep.

The remainder of this chapter explains what I mean, so if you can spare the time, let's walk together for a while.

I am the bored little boy in the pew who has spent much of the past thirty years in pulpits and platforms on every continent. Sports arenas, circus tents, theatres, cinemas, churches, chapels and night clubs; from the back of a boat to a shopping precinct or two; Canterbury Cathedral and the Royal Albert Hall. That adds up to a lot of time, a lot of sermons and a lot of people.

So what happened?

It's a long story – much of which is too personal to tell. But here are some signposts that I have passed along the way. They have become important to me the longer I have journeyed because they mark the path I have taken.

Calling

There is a difference between speaking and preaching and I think it's down to calling and gifting. I have met lots of people who can give a talk with some good insights and I have met others who have a natural talent to communicate. But preaching is more than having the gift of the gab – to coin a phrase. It is a spiritual gift and the service (ministry) of preaching relies on the call of Christ on a person's life.

I often think back to Jeremiah, who reached such a low point in his life that he decided to stop preaching – only to discover that the word of God became a fire in his body that he couldn't extinguish.[1] He was called to deliver God's word and the issue was more about his willingness to obey rather than talent.

I look back to the time that God called me to preach – it was no sudden thing but rather a gradual awakening to the overwhelming truth that his hand was resting on my life and that I was being called to a task of inestimable privilege. I didn't want to be a preacher; I simply discovered that is what I was being called to do. There have been many times when I would have taken another job – but that would have been to step out of the will of God.

So the first question I always put to someone asking about preaching is simply this: Do you have a sense of God's call on your life to be a preacher of the Gospel? If not, then don't bother. If so, then give it your best attention.

Gifting

It is difficult within the limitations of a brief chapter to explain all that I would like to say about spiritual gifting. So I will discipline myself to be brief. The ability to preach and teach is a gift of God's Spirit in the life of a Christian disciple. I am conscious (deeply so) that I have been loaned a precious gift that is received on trust. The skill is not mine, although I am called to steward, nurture and develop it for all I am worth. But I live constantly with the knowledge that I could wake tomorrow morning and the gift could be gone. That makes me very careful.

Mentoring

As I look back in my life I am aware of how many helped me along the road, not simply in terms of discipleship but also in developing the gift of preaching. When I left theological college back in 1975 I spent five years working with a team of evangelists. This was an important time of formation for me. They were all quality men who had a passion for the Gospel and for some reason they took a brash twenty-three-year-old under their wing as they undertook church-based missions all over Britain.

That was my apprenticeship: school assemblies, classroom discussions and endless coffee mornings, combined with working alongside a team of skilled preachers. Peter Anderson, John Blanchard, Derek Cleave, Derek Cook, Dave Pope all mentored me in an informal, unstructured way. They showed me the truth of Phillips Brookes' classic definition: 'Preaching is the bringing of truth through personality.'[2] God uses different personalities to communicate truth, and understanding this liberates us to be who we are, rather than trying to be anyone else.

The best thing anyone called to preach can do is to study as many preachers as they possibly can (and that includes preachers of previous generations). If possible, listen to their tapes, read their sermons and learn from their good points as well as the bad. Discern the great communicators among the good ones and think hard about what they teach you. Then go and work hard at allowing the timeless truth of Scripture to come through your own personality to the glory of God.

Passion

Preparing to write this, I made a list of some preachers that I heard as a child – John Stott, Martyn Lloyd-Jones, Billy Graham, Roger Forster, David Pawson, Tom Rees, George B. Duncan. Being a son of the manse I came in contact with men of this calibre. (And that bored ten-year-old at the start of the chapter took in more then most reckoned.)

Then, as I grew in my faith, I had the opportunity to hear others and I listened with greater intent: David Watson, R. T. Kendall, Alan Redpath, Roy Clements, Sidlow Baxter, Dick Lucas and Paul Rees. And among my own contemporaries people such as Eric Delve, Nick Cuthbert and Clive Calver were hugely influential. The emergence of Spring Harvest opened the door to a stream of people from outside the UK context; Tony Campolo, Ajith Fernando, Elisabeth Elliott, Floyd McClung, Luis Palau, Leighton Ford, John Wimber and Josh McDowell are just a few names that spring to mind.

But from an early age I learned to spot those who had passion and those who didn't. Please understand, I am not mistaking passion for shouting and waving your arms about. Some of the above couldn't do either to save their lives. What I am describing is the capacity to preach from the heart to the heart.

This came home to me in a curious way. When my four sons were small we enjoyed a boys' day out with a visit to Old Trafford (the home of Manchester United) and Anfield (the ground of Liverpool FC). It was a great day as we toured behind the scenes of these shrines to English football. On our way home I asked my children which was the better of the two tours. Manchester United won hands down and I was fascinated by their childlike logic. The two tour guides were the deciding factor for them. The man at Liverpool was polite and informative but, according to my sons, they could tell he was doing a job because he was paid to do it. But the guide at Old Trafford was something else. He'd grown up a stone's throw from the ground and had been a lifelong Manchester United supporter. When he quoted statistics of victories won he positively glowed and – according to my lads – he would have done the job for nothing.

The light came on for me as I reflected on the penetrating insight of four small boys. What they had seen was passion, borne of a conviction that what was being communicated came from the centre of the man's being.

That is never more true than when it comes to preaching. The word 'witness' is widely used in the New Testament – the Greek word is *martus*, from which we derive the English word 'martyr' because of those whose witness to Christ led to their death.[3]

If you can't preach with passion then don't bother to preach at all. And the way to discover and nurture that passion is through personal discipleship that challenges you to listen hard to your own sermons.

Charles Spurgeon – the great Baptist preacher of the Victorian era – used to say about choosing a Bible passage or verse to preach on that it was not so much a case of selecting something but rather a verse choosing you. Once it has gripped your heart and challenged you at the centre of your being, then it will do the same as you seek to communicate it to others. These are wise words that bear careful reflection.

Humility

A long time ago I came across a quote from the Scottish theologian James Denney. I have long since lost the source but the words come back to me regularly – often in the final few seconds before I get up to preach to a congregation. 'You cannot at one and the same time convince people how clever you are – and what a great Saviour Jesus is.' When I am reminded of that quotation I feel as if I am called to make a renewed choice. Which is it to be?

It was Billy Graham who said that people in Christian leadership who made a mess of their ministry usually fell because of one (or more) of three reasons – money, sex or pride. Experience shows he is absolutely correct. The first two are obvious, the temptation of money has wrecked many ministries and so has the whole area of illicit sexual relationships. But pride is not so obvious. It manifests itself in a host of ways. Preachers can start to believe their own publicity, react with hostility to any criticism, lack relationships that offer accountability and begin to see themselves as a special case where the normal rules of Christian conduct don't apply.

Hudson Taylor, a missionary pioneer of a previous generation, accomplished much for the Kingdom of God. His son was asked the reason for his father's fruitful life and answered: 'He remained small enough for God to use.'

There is so much more I could say, but I leave these five signposts as important markers that have helped my journey.

One last thing.

That small boy in the pew has discovered that to be called to preach the Gospel of Christ is better than anything. I often feel like Moses' mother, who ended up being paid to look after her own child – something she would have done for no more than love.[4]

NOTES
1. Jeremiah 20:8–9.
2. Phillips Brooks, *Lectures on Preaching* (delivered at the Divinity School of Yale College), (London: H. R. Allenson, 1895), (5).
3. See Acts 22:20, Revelation 2:13 and 17:6.
4. See Exodus 2:8–9.

5

James D. G. Dunn

REFLECTIONS OF A
LOCAL PREACHER

*James D. G. Dunn has been preaching for nearly 50 years. He read theo-
logy and trained for Church of Scotland ministry in Glasgow. He served
in a Glasgow parish for one year and as Chaplain to Overseas Students
in Edinburgh for two years, before his appointment as Lecturer in New
Testament at the University of Nottingham in 1970, and subsequently
as Lightfoot Professor of Divinity in the University of Durham (from
1982). In Nottingham his family attended the local church, which happened to be Methodist, and since then he has served as a Local Preacher
in local Methodist circuits. He has written more than twenty books on
New Testament themes. He retired in 2003. In 2004 he received a
Certificate for 40 years' service as a Local Preacher of the Methodist
Church (in fact, it was the fortieth anniversary of his licensing as a
minister of the Church of Scotland).*

I began my preaching career as a seventeen-year-old. I had just
finished school and was spending the summer as a porter in a
hotel on the Island of Bute. Somehow it had been discovered that
I was preparing to train for the Church of Scotland ministry. But
it still came as something of a shock when I was approached by
a local church to lead a service. Knowing that this was a challenge I would have to meet sooner or later, I agreed, though with

much trepidation. To ensure that I wouldn't dry up, in case my mind went blank, I wrote out absolutely everything, including 'Let us worship God' and 'Let us pray'. I survived, and still have the service 'script' in my shoebox of personal mementoes.

That service and sermon were the first of many. I suppose I have preached at and/or led a service of worship on average about once a month – that's nearly 600 times, on a rough calculation, since I started. So it may be of interest to others, as it certainly is to me, if I now look back over these years and note how much my preaching has changed or developed, before commenting on how I now go about my sermon preparation.

Quite soon after that first service I had gained enough confidence to dispense with a full manuscript, for sermon and prayers. I soon realised that I needed to maintain eye contact with the worshipping congregation. A sense of rapport with the congregation (or lecture audience) always has been of major importance for me. I need to be sensitive to how (or whether) the congregation/audience is hearing what I am trying to say. Such sensitivity enables me to vary pace and tone and volume, to react appropriately when the congregation/audience is with me or is obviously not, to insert a clarificatory addition, or repeat a point, or abbreviate a longer section, or to throw in a humorous aside, and so on.

To achieve such a sense of rapport and to be able to adapt the presentation accordingly has always been for me one of the exhilarating aspects of preaching; it becomes a living encounter with those addressed. In that sense, I believe that a preacher has to be something of an orator or actor, or at least to develop their skills. In essence, the challenge before both actor and orator is to 'persuade' the listeners of the importance and significance of the message, to draw the listeners in to experience for themselves the personal or existential import of what is being said. In that sense I do not hesitate to think of preaching as a kind of 'performance' (it was never a surprise to me that my younger daughter chose to become an actress). Not that I am very good at 'illustrations': I rely more on vividness of vocabulary and vigour of speech, a style very much dependent on 'rapport' and 'performance'. Need I add that I have no desire to reduce preaching to a merely rhetorical exercise, and I don't need reminding of what Paul says in 1 Corinthians 2:1–4 about speaking 'not with plausible words of wisdom, but with a demonstration of the Spirit and of power' (NRSV). But a good preacher soon learns that there are 'tricks of the trade', without which preaching may miss the mark, and I remind those who cite Paul at this point that Paul's very denial that he used such 'tricks' is one of the oldest of the 'tricks'! That said, Paul's key point remains crucial: unless the Spirit of God speaks through the preacher's words, however good or bad the 'performance', there is little likelihood of the sermon making a 'gospel impact'.

I now regularly preach only from notes. For the last 12 or so years (post-computer) I have developed the practice of setting out my notes on a single A4 page, set sideways and formatted in two columns. With some slight trimming by scissors the resulting two smallish pages fit neatly into my 'preaching Bible' (presented to me when I was licensed as a preacher in Glasgow Cathedral in 1964). Experience has taught me that such notes are usually sufficient for a 20–25-minute sermon. On very formal occasions, when time is strictly limited, the notes will be more extensive, though I try as much as possible to avoid being too tied to a manuscript.

Following similar logic, I regularly pray in a worship service extempore, though with the theme and structure of the prayer thought through beforehand. In this way I can be more sensitive to the mood of the congregation and any late information about it, and adapt structure and content accordingly.

Being brought up and trained in the Reformed (Church of Scotland) tradition, I inherited a very high appreciation of the place and role of the sermon in a worship service. In typically Reformed architecture, the pulpit is central and stands above the communion table – the Word above the Sacrament, the Sacrament as the Word made visible. And typically in traditional Reformed worship the sermon functions as the climax of the service, with only the concluding hymn and benediction to follow. I followed this practice during my years in Scotland. But when we settled in England, in 1970, we went to the local church (Presbyterian churches were fewer and further between), which happened to be Methodist, and so I became a Methodist and soon began to function as a Local Preacher. Quite quickly I began to see value in a different order of service, where the sermon was more at the centre, and where offering, intercessions (and church notices!) could serve as some kind of (congregational) response to the Word.

Occasionally I have experimented with congregational feed-back and discussion of the sermon as part of the service, but this has rarely been very practicable. Here too I am influenced by Paul, who never saw the delivery of a word from God as an act in itself but insisted that some within the congregation, or the congregation itself, should exercise discernment as to the significance and bearing of what had been said and as part of the congregation's gathering for worship (1 Cor. 14:29; 1 Thess. 5:19–22). I still wish we could devise service structures where such further discussion could be possible. In the same way I have been glad occasionally to be able to take part in some team planning of services and to pre-discuss the sermon. Paul's vision of the congregation operating as the body of Christ (Rom. 12:6–8; 1 Cor. 12) has always thrilled and challenged me, with all sharing in ministry (a much broader, more profound concept of ministry) in mutual interdependence, and grace being corporately chan-nelled to the whole rather than being overly (or exclusively) dependent on the insight and preparation of one individual.

The main point, however, is that I can no longer regard the rest of the worship as simply an adjunct to or setting for the sermon. For me the service is a whole, and my prayer is always that the congregation may benefit from the service, that is, from different parts of the service as God may speak to them through hymn, or prayer, or choir, or sermon, or whatever. I cherish the memory of the testimony of an ordinand recollecting her call to ministry coming in a service which I led: as I was preening myself, she added, 'Not through his sermon but through one of the hymns'! My objective on this point, then, is to prepare a 'whole service', with hymns and readings and prayers reinforcing one another, not slavishly, of course, but with the awareness that a message expressed in different forms is the more likely to be effective in its impact.

My Reformed inheritance also taught me the importance of the sermon as a means of teaching the congregation. A typical expression of this tradition is the sermon series, where across a three-month (or longer, sometimes much longer) period the sermons in the series will expound a biblical book from beginning to end in sequence. Conscious of how impoverished and wholly inadequate Christian education is in this country, the sermon seemed to me the best (perhaps the only effective) way of instructing whole congregations in the Scriptures and great themes of the Christian faith. To that end, in early days I would plan to preach on such great texts and themes and try to pack as much as I could into the 20–25 minutes allotted. How dense these sermons must have been. What spiritual indigestion I must have caused! Looking back at notes of old sermons I see that in several cases the later treatments of such themes omitted up to half of the original content or divided the material into two (or more) sermons. The sparser treatment, of course, allowed me to elaborate and illustrate the fewer points being made, and thus, I hope, to 'drive' them home more effectively.

I have also revised my view of the sermon as a means of teaching. There is an important difference between a lecture or lesson or Bible study and a sermon. The former are much more suitable for sustained teaching. The sermon is too brief for that (as I soon found), and anyway has a broader function, including the ministry of exhortation and encouragement. The prophecy that occurred in earliest Christian worship, of which the New Testament speaks (1 Cor. 14), is sometimes identified with preaching. And insofar as prophecy is distinct from teaching, there is something in that. But rightly understood, biblical 'prophecy' is too spontaneous, words given immediately by the

Spirit, for the identification to be complete. And the preparation which today's preachers typically have to give their sermons aligns their role more closely to that of the teacher than the prophet. Moreover, as already indicated, I have moved away from the 'preacher as prophet' model. It builds too much on the Old Testament idea of the individual prophet as the sole mouth-piece of God's Spirit and channel of revelation and grace. It does not take seriously enough the New Testament (Paul's in particular) recognition of the congregation as a whole as the body of Christ, of ministry operating in multiform ways, and of grace funnelling to individual members through the interactions of the many.

Despite these reservations, as a professional theologian, I often find myself using the sermon to provide a modest amount of teaching, in regard to a particular passage or theme. From the first it has seemed to me wise to give the sermon a structure, rather than developing a theme continuously through the 20–25 minutes without discernible breaks. An unstructured sermon (or lecture) is much harder to grasp with the mind and retain in the memory. So I have always been a 'three-pointer'. Again, not slavishly, of course; my last sermon had four sub-divisions. But three points, with each point developed briefly but appropriately, is about right for a typical sermon of this length. Three points ensures that some at least of the richness or complexity of the topic can be demonstrated. And three points allows a progression in the sermon, which helps to sustain interest. The primary objective, need it be said, is to let the text or topic unfold in a way that is most natural to it and elucidatory of it. But that will usually (not always) mean a structured sermon, and in my experience the simplest framework on which to hang one's insights and reflections is the threefold one.

A fourth development in my preaching practice has been rather later in emerging. For the majority of my career as a preacher I have tended to choose my own text or theme and preach on that. My logic, I guess, was that I had something to say on this text or that theme, and that I should use the opportunity given me as a preacher to expound it. So sermons, for example, on 'Fellowship' and 'Grace', 'Holy Spirit' and 'Wisdom' did the rounds. My annotations at the head of some notes indicate that I used the notes ten or more times. I must have preached on passages like John 1:1–18 and the Good Samaritan many times and in many contexts. Not that any two sermons were exactly the same; the 'performance' character of each preaching has meant that the same notes were elaborated differently on each occasion. The notes, often with paragraphs scored out, and improvements pencilled in, provide a less than adequate record of my preaching on that theme. And on some themes I have several different versions of the same sermon, or reminders that in some cases, where I had studied a theme or text intensively, the subject could be preached either in summary fashion or in several 'bites'.

The shoebox record file also contains, buried deep down, records of early attempts to tackle texts and themes on which my views have changed (I would prefer to say 'matured'). By which I mean, of course, that my insights into these topics have sharpened and my understanding of these topics has been deepened. Here, too, I rather cringe to have to recall more naive expositions (as they now seem to me), and wince at the thought of what I put some congregations through. On the other hand, some of the early insights given me have remained with me and still provide important elements of my current preaching. As part of a major exercise in my second year of Divinity in Glasgow (simultaneously training at Trinity College for the Church of Scotland ministry) I had to write an exegesis of John 1:1–18 and to prepare a sermon on it, a sermon which was actually preached. The insights I gained from engaging in close exegesis of the passage gave me a sermon outline which, apart from being abbreviated, I can still use today.

The main development at this point has been my shift (from about 1990, but spasmodic before then) from choosing my own theme or topic to following the texts set for the Sunday in question by the standard lectionary. I had always recognised the value of the lectionary, in that it covered the full range of the Bible, including, of course, texts and passages which I might never light upon when choosing my own topic. So, it made good sense to take one or other of the set passages as the basis for leading the congregation's meditation. 'The lectionary discipline' also means that difficult passages cannot be avoided. And such passages should be tackled. Bible readers inevitably come across such passages in their reading and most need to be helped to confront and cope with such passages. Moreover, as a professional student of the New Testament, if I avoided such passages, by not using the lectionary, what kind of exercise of my gifts and my responsibility as a teacher was that? The point has been illustrated for me in the last two years, when 'lectionary discipline' made me face the fact that I had never preached on the Transfiguration or on the Parable of the Unjust Judge. But what had driven the point home to me with inescapable force was a sermon I had heard some years ago on John 8, in which it was simply taken for granted that John's talk of 'the Jews' warranted a very negative Christian view of Judaism. Such a passage should not be avoided, but it requires some careful explanation of the historical circumstances behind John's language and consequent limitation of John's references to 'the Jews'. Here was a case where, as a New Testament scholar, were I preaching on a Sunday when that reading was set, I had a positive duty to take that prescribed reading and 'set the record straight', and so help to counter the often still virulent strains of Christian anti-Judaism.

I should perhaps add that using the lectionary became for me a very good self-discipline. On not a few occasions, prior to this development in my preaching practice, it was convenient for me to take the easy way out, and use an old sermon/service. With a demanding full-time job and a very active family, pressure of time made the convenient get-out very attractive and too often unavoidable. And as a local preacher, or invited to guest preach, of course, I did not have the challenge of having to stand before the same congregation Sunday after Sunday, when it would have been impossible to use old material. On reflection, however, this weakness of Methodist worship (where the worship leader and preacher is unlikely to be the same person on consecutive Sundays) became a further reason to adopt 'the lectionary discipline'. For if each of the different preachers (ministers or local preachers) filling the pulpit on a succession of Sundays were to follow the lectionary readings, then at least it would provide some of the continuity of reading and theme which Methodist congregations often find lacking in their worship experience.

So, how do I now go about my sermon preparation? This was a question which a student minister at Wesley Study Centre, Durham, put to me as part of an intriguing project he had taken on. We met several times, he quizzed me before and after a couple of sermons, and attended the services at which they were delivered. It was my participation in this project which sparked off much of the train of thought followed through above. In what follows I recall much (perhaps most) of what I said to him.

Preparation ideally and usually begins for me two or three weeks before the appointed Sunday (earlier if the service in view is a 'big' one). I first check the lectionary readings set for that Sunday. The hope is always that one or other of the readings will spark off a subject or theme for the sermon (and service); the hope has failed to be realised only once in recent years. My attention tends to focus on either the Gospel or the Epistle (including Acts and Revelation), although, being aware that the traditional homily is almost always on the Gospel, I pay particular attention to the Epistle. All I am looking for at that point is some sense that there is going to be subject matter for the sermon/service.

I then, in effect, pop the passage(s) into my subconscious, and during the intervening time pull it out once or twice for fresh scrutiny. My experience has been that the most fruitfully generative times have been in the course of the night, when I may wake up for some time (often half-conscious), or wake early, an hour or so before getting-up time. Again and again I have found that a few minutes' reflection has given me a theme and structure, typically a three-point framework, with indications of how the framework can be filled out. Amazingly, I have almost always been able to recall the framework in my (fully) waking hours. And again typically, during the week before the Sunday, with some further reflection, while walking into or from town, or in a quiet moment during an evening, I have been able to fill out each element of the framework (the three points) to provide the content and shape necessary for the occasion in view. I realise that there may be some important corollaries for our understanding of how God's Spirit works through and from within us (through the unconscious) in what I am testifying to.

Normally, on the Thursday evening before the service I will sketch on paper the outline of the sermon which has been taking shape in my mind. Readings are usually as per the lectionary, though I may replace one of the supporting readings with one more suitable to the theme being drawn from the others. Hymns are chosen – usually only four, since I try to avoid the impression of a 'hymn-prayer sandwich'. The topic for a children's address, if required, is wrestled with, if possible in consultation with my wife (Meta), whose experience as a nursery teacher and junior Sunday school leader taught me all the most important things I ever learned about speaking to younger children. And some preliminary thought is given to the prayers. All this takes place in consultation with one or more of the stewards of the chapel where I am 'planned' to be. For other, 'big' occasions, of course, such consultation is completed far earlier.

Typically, I give the first part of Saturday morning to putting the sermon outline into the computer format described earlier and to finalising the order of service. Hymns are communicated to the church steward and readers asked for, if I have not already done so in response to a request from the steward to fit in with the church's timetable.

On Sunday morning I get up earlier than usual (for a Sunday) and spend 40–45 minutes in preparation, going over the service from beginning to end, getting clear in my mind the structure and elements of the prayers and of the children's address (if required), and 'preaching' the sermon from the notes.

In all this, I am conscious that I have said nothing about my own praying as part of the preparation. This is partly because few of my prayers today are formal (eyes-shut, head-bowed) prayers. Praying for me is more a matter of doing things, in this case particularly my sermon/service preparation, conscious of my dependence on God and his Spirit. In the course of this many an actual prayer will be verbalised: that is, on particular points I will ask for help, for guidance, for a sharper insight, and so on; specific elements and formulations I will consciously hold before God for his approval (or otherwise). I used to spend the Sunday morning preparation period on my knees, but prefer now to sit comfortably on a sofa, quietly and prayerfully running through the service and sermon, often retracing my steps to ensure that I have some connection or illustration or point clear to myself (if it's not clear to myself, I can hardly hope to make it clear to others).

The interval before the service (I rarely accept other than morning appointments) is one of the most difficult for me. The preparation period has set me in a frame of mind, focused, concentrated, open (I trust) to God's Spirit – running over elements of the service while showering or dressing or in the car – so that I must appear to my wife and others as somewhat detached from what's going on around (classic example of the absent-minded professor).

In the vestry I am almost always nervous. And glad to be so: the weight of responsibility to lead God's people in worship worthy of their/our God should be a pressing burden; the privilege and possibility to speak a word from God to his people is awesome. I never want to forget that or to fail to feel that. I can manage friendly conversations with stewards who like to chat and/or who feel they are helping put the preacher at ease. And, of course, various things need to be checked, orders of service distributed, last-minute items for prayer communicated. But for the rest I am content to be quiet and to sustain the calmness of soul which the preparation period gave me.

After the service – usually already earlier, once the prayers of intercession are complete – I begin to feel a substantial sense of relief. Relief that I have been able to carry through the service and the sermon as it had been given to me and I had constructed it. Relief that the extempore elements had gone as well as they had and at such degree of rapport as I had experienced. Relief, I suppose, similar to that experienced by the actor or orator after a successful performance. Sometimes there are traces of euphoria, when several members of the congregation express appreciation for the service, and in terms you know they mean. At other times the mere formality of the handshakes leaves you wondering, occasionally depressed. But I have learned to place little weight on either response. I have known too many occasions when I felt really good about the way a service had gone, only to be deflated by lack of response from the congregation or some sharply insightful observations from my wife (when she has accompanied me). But I have also known several occasions when I felt that the service had gone badly, only to learn later that this one and that one had been greatly helped by the service. Thanks be to God that he can convey such treasure through such weak vessels.

I see now that I am next scheduled to lead a service and preach in four weeks' time (just after returning from 17 days abroad). Ah! First Sunday in Advent. That should set the juices flowing and the wheels in motion. Lead me, Lord!

6

Susan Durber

MY PREACHING JOURNEY

Susan Durber is a minister of the United Reformed Church, now serving two churches in Oxford. She has a PhD on the parables of Jesus. She was a major contributor to Worship: from the United Reformed Church, *the latest URC service book, and has published work on preaching, biblical studies and prayers.*

When I was a small child, my grandmother used to say that I would be a novelist. My brother said almost nothing until he was three, but he would listen to me and I would somehow tell my family what he wanted to say but didn't. My grandmother watched and listened as I told him endless stories and wove narratives from my toys. Any toys could be coaxed into service. Even when I was given Lego bricks, I would use them to make people and houses and tell stories with them, so they might as well have been dolls or characters in a book. My family was not bookish and I had only a small number of story books, but the ones I had were well read and dog-eared. And even my own life I turned into a narrative. Walking along the pavement, or riding silently in the back of the car, I would turn myself into a character in a book and narrate my own story in my head. My grand-mother was convinced that I was going to write novels. But she

was wrong. I was not to be the new Jane Austen. I was preparing
to be a preacher.

I was also growing up as a girl, and a rather conventional girl
in some ways. My mother thought short hair best, and in the
1960s it was fashionable, but I dreamt of long hair. The princesses
in the stories I loved had long hair and I had little-girl dreams of
weddings and party dresses and jewels. I played happily for
hours, nursing my dolls, constructing homes and carriages for
them, dressing and undressing, loving and tending them. I
enjoyed school and I loved the opportunities it brought for
hearing, writing and telling stories, and for the power it gave me
to use words and letters to create my own world. I had not much
idea of what women could do in the world beyond raising
children and looking beautiful, but I knew what pleasure words
and stories brought to me and I wanted somehow to find a place
where I could do that all my days.

And I was a profoundly religious child. I found Sunday school
rather trying, though I dutifully accumulated coloured stamps
for attendance and prizes for reading the Bible. But something in
me responded to the interiors of churches, the smell of churches
and, more than anything, the sound of hymns more ancient than
modern and the drone of the organ. The world my father drove
us through on Sunday afternoon trips to the seaside and the
countryside also gave me a sense of the holiness and mystery of
the world, especially the rolling sea or the sweep of clouds across
the sky. Something in these glimpses of the world filled me with
a sense of longing and of what I came to know as 'the beyondness
of things'.

In and between these three things I discovered the first faint
echoes of a vocation, or at least, a sense of what I wanted to do as
my part in the world's life. But it took me a while to get there,
even though the first intimations came early, because I could not
see at first how these things were connected to each other. When
I was very young, about eight years old, I began to sense that
God might be calling me to serve in the Church in some way. I
was worshipping then in the Church of England and I thought I

wanted to be a priest. This was in the 1960s and I hadn't noticed, or at least hadn't thought about, the fact that all the priests I had ever seen were men. But I knew that I should do what the priest did: take the service, sing the responses and, more than anything, preach. Unusually, I should think, I used to look forward to the occasional services when the children of the Sunday school could stay in the service and listen to the sermon. I enjoyed it and marvelled at the thoughtfulness of a sermon, the luxury of pondering ideas and searching for understanding. And I loved the space the sermon offered to find peace from the apparently ceaseless activity of childhood learning – a beautiful space. I knew that I wanted to create such spaces myself and began to prepare myself to do it. I knew I would have to be patient. And I was. I studied carefully at school, the right O levels and A levels, Oxbridge entrance in Religious Studies and then a Theology degree at Oxford. And during this time I had joined a United Reformed Church, where the sermons seemed, to me at least, to be longer and more intellectually demanding (I would sit in my place in the choir taking notes!) and where, so I had heard, it was possible for women to be ordained as ministers.

But in this time of earnest preparation for what I believed was my vocation, there were parts of me which I carefully and gently placed to one side, suppressed perhaps. I learned that sermons were full of ideas and carefully worked argument, that sermons were to be delivered almost like lectures, though often with some raising of the voice, and that sermons were spoken from a generalised kind of human experience to humanity at large. I found such sermons challenging and intellectually stimulating – they fed my mind and, to a great extent, my spirit. I enjoyed listening to them and thinking hard about them. But I had forgotten the catch of the breath and the lump in the throat that I had sometimes known as a sense of the reality of God in my childhood. And I had forgotten the power of stories and the longing to write them and tell them – and how to use words for beauty and longing, as I had once done so readily. And I had left behind, too, my sense of myself as a girl and of my life as a girl's life. I longed to join the guild of male preachers and to take on their styles, just as I knew that I should one day wear a Geneva gown and the plain white tabs of a preacher. I continued to read novels and poems, to write short pieces and to delight in words. And I lived my life, a woman's life, in a world whose shape was cast by men, but rarely spoke of this or acknowledged its particular challenges and graces. And despite knowing every novel of E. M. Forster almost by heart, I did not heed his message 'only connect', and so did not bring together the greatest loves and passions of my life in pursuing my vocation. I became a minister and preached faithfully Sunday by Sunday, but my heroes were the male preachers I had learned to admire and the styles I adopted without thinking were the styles that they, and I, had inherited. But I began, despite the busyness of my days and the demands of ministry, to sense that I had not yet found my own voice and that there was something as yet unformed about my life as a preacher.

Then, over some years, several things happened which helped me to connect the gifts and the life that God had given me with my preaching. And I began to speak with a different voice. My awakening came through men and through women, through lived experience and through philosophical reflection, through a blissful letting go and through sheer hard work. And the process still continues as life unfolds and as the adventure of thinking and learning, creating and encountering goes on.

In my initial ministerial training there had been little overt reflection on the task of preaching, and even a positive resistance to such reflection. Preaching was imagined, it seemed, to be an almost natural process, caught rather than taught. But a spell spent in a seminary in the United States opened the world of 'homiletics' to me, and I discovered a whole host of preachers who, like me, loved and treasured words and who knew, more than I did, how to use words to evoke that beat of the heart and lifting of the spirit that I remembered from childhood as an intimation of the holy. I warmed to the writings of the Jesuit preacher Walter Burghardt. In his book *Preaching: the Art and the*

Craft, he wrote about the long hours he would spend crafting and tending his words, of how he wanted to evoke something in his hearers and not simply to describe or argue, and of how he used everything he lived and read as food for his soul and for his hearers. I knew at last that I had found a key to the locked door I stared at as I prepared to preach. I longed to do what he could do, and was thrilled to find that it was permissible and possible to think of preaching in these ways. And then I also discovered, wide-eyed with recognition, the work of Frederick Buechner, an American novelist and preacher from the Presbyterian tradition who writes beautifully and powerfully of life and of God. I was fascinated to find someone who writes novels, theology *and* sermons and who moves easily from one to the other. He was, and is, little known in the UK, partly at least because he has a fear of flying and so rarely leaves the United States. And perhaps also because his writing is so rooted in everyday life that it is less easy to transfer to a different context. But I find his story and his work fascinating and compelling and I continue to read everything I can find that he's written. Whether novels, autobiography, pen-portraits of Bible characters or sermons themselves, his work shows how to use words well to evoke, convey, transport and connect. Buechner has written a book called *The Sacred Journey: a memoir of early days.* He begins the book with this stunning paragraph:

> all theology, like all fiction, is at its heart autobiography … what a theologian is doing essentially is examining as honestly as he can the rough-and-tumble of his or her own experience with all its ups and downs, its mysteries and loose ends, and expressing … the truths about human life and about God that he believes he had found implicit there. … If God speaks to us at all in this world, if God speaks anywhere, it is into our personal lives that he speaks. Someone we love dies, say. Some unforeseen act of kindness or cruelty touches the heart or makes the blood run cold. We fail a friend, or a friend fails us, and we are appalled at the

capacity we have for estranging the very people in our lives we need the most. Or maybe nothing extraordinary happens at all – just one day following another, helter-skelter, in the manner of days. We sleep and dream. We wake. We work. We remember and forget. We have fun and are depressed. And into the thick of it, or out of the thick of it, at moments of even the most humdrum of our days, God speaks. (Buechner, 1982, pp. 1–2)

One of his most influential books is, as it happens, a book about preaching – *Telling the Truth: The Gospel as Tragedy, Comedy and Fairy Tale*. It's a book I constantly return to for encouragement and inspiration in the task of preaching and one which never fails to move and strengthen me. Buechner knows, as we all know deep down, that preachers are all as heavy laden under what he calls 'the burden of being human' as their hearers and that it is from this place that we must preach the Gospel. He writes,

if preachers … are to say anything that really matters to anyone including themselves, they must say it not just to the public part of us that considers interesting thoughts about the Gospel and how to preach it, but to the private, inner part too, to the part of us all where our dreams come from, both our good dreams and our bad dreams, the inner part where thoughts mean less than images, elucidation less than evocation, where our concern is less with how the Gospel is to be preached than with what the Gospel is and what it is to us. They must address themselves to the fullness of who we are and to the emptiness too, the emptiness where grace and peace belong. (Buechner, 1977, p. 4)

Buechner teaches us that preaching the Gospel is not just about telling the truth, but telling the truth in love, which means telling it with concern for the people it is being told to, to feel what it is like to live inside the skins of other people. And here I found that my love of the stories other people tell of their lives, the stories I heard in pastoral encounters and through novels and films and all sorts of narratives, these helped me to tell the truth in love. Buechner gave me permission at last to be interested in the unfolding story of my own life and of others' lives, to read words that were true to human experience, whether in poetry or prose, and to draw such words into my work as a preacher. I recognised that my love and admiration for narrative, and the power of words to evoke, describe and heal were not after all things I needed only for my spare time, but were a source for preaching. Buechner sees part of the work of preaching to be to 'put words to both the wonder and horror of the world', to use words to explain, expound and exhort – yes – but also to use them to evoke, to set us dreaming, to stir in us intuitions and memories that we long for, but hardly know that we long for. Buechner invites any preacher to draw on 'nothing fancier than the poetry of his (sic) own life' and to use words to make the lives of all who hear 'transparent to the truth'. I read Buechner's own sermons, I read his novels, and I listened to tapes of him speaking, and I understood what he meant. I began to find my own ways of using words well, or at least better, and I began to draw on the poetry of my own life. Not, I must add, to parade my own experience in sermons, but to allow my own life to open up to me the mystery of the lives of others.

My CV looks astonishingly boring – not much more than being a student and being a minister. But like all apparently ordinary lives, my own has its extraordinary qualities too – as I have lived through being ordained, giving birth to a daughter, loving scandalously and deeply, living through divorce, loving a woman whom I nursed until she died in my arms, and so much more which it would be too much to say. And there are not only happenings and events, but longings, feelings, fears and pains, bliss and hopes – which now again I see as intuitions of God or at least of that mysterious 'beyondness' to which I hope to testify. I began in my preaching to bring to life the stories of the Bible, even the stories behind the pieces that are not obviously narrative, to tell them again in words which would make them live for my hearers and which would show them, rather than persuade them, how these stories are indeed holy. And my sermons began to be touched again by the real power of the Gospel to be good news and to bring something of the beat of the heart and the catch of the breath that is a sign of the possibility of God. The 'passion' and so much creativity had been removed from me, slowly but decisively, by the rigorous processes of my training for ministry, but I had found it again – and in a way which I knew could be a gentle craft rather than an uncontrolled explosion, and which could be used in the service of God's people.

Alongside this rediscovery of the power of language and of a kind of suppressed longing in me to tell human stories, I discovered something else about my distinctive voice. It was the voice of a woman. In the popular BBC television series about a woman vicar, *The Vicar of Dibley*, Geraldine tells her congregation in an early sermon that they should not be afraid that everything will be changed because the vicar is a woman. She reassures them that the 'hymns' will not become 'hers'. This reflects one response to women's preaching – to say that it makes no difference at all who is speaking. So, it is sometimes argued that the 'gospel' is unchanging and objective, the truth is the truth belonging to God and not to the person who speaks it. Women preachers will preach just as men have preached and in wearing the preaching gown, tabs or stole, they will naturally wear also the forms and styles of the preacher's voice and their gender will not, or even should not, make any difference. Another approach is to argue that women will naturally and obviously preach in a different way, that there is an essential difference. Carol M. Noren, in her book *The Woman in the Pulpit*, argues that women's grammar and syntax tend to be different from men's, that women have their own characteristic speech patterns, that they have 'a predilection towards relational or social language', poetic, evocative language and adverbs.

But as I had learned to be a preacher, it hardly ever occurred to me that it might, or could, make a difference that I was a woman. My pulpit heroes were men and I had learned to emulate those I judged the best. But there came a time when I began to think about the question of my gender, and to ask what it meant for preaching. As I reflected on the raw material of my own life's experience as the place in which God was made real, it dawned on me that my experience was that of a woman. When my daughter was born, the sheer fact of my being a woman could no longer be hidden even from myself. I was confronted with the lived experience of a woman's life and it was my own. I also began to learn from feminist friends and to read for myself the sacred canon of feminism. I learned that being a 'woman' is not simply a natural thing, but is always already 'made' or constructed within the world we make with our words and our ways of thinking. I saw that being a woman in our culture was not something that could be left out of thought, and neither was it something that had an essential and immediately available meaning. I came to see what a powerful force for the understanding of women was the faith tradition to which I belonged and which I proclaimed, and of how there was some power here which I could properly seize as a woman preacher. With some wonderful and faithful friends, I began to preach self-consciously and deliberately from the particular experience of being a woman. With others among my friends, I began to choose the often forgotten Bible texts which told stories of women's lives (albeit from an androcentric perspective), to speak from among the women I knew and whose stories I began to hear in new ways, and to recognise that my words from the pulpit could be part of a reforming of women's lives – now alongside what I had imagined was universal human experience, but was actually male experience generalised.

In preaching, as with other discourses in which women speak, gender is not irrelevant, it is not an essential given (it is not obvious that all women will naturally preach with the same voice which is always and uniformly different from the male voice), and neither is it purely a social construct or within our power to determine and use. But just as in other areas of life, women are discovering how to take their lived reality as a resource and to form new and liberating visions of what it means to be a woman, so this can happen when a woman preaches. I began to believe that it could happen when I preach. Preaching is an 'embodied practice' and a 'performance' and may become a place where women find and claim a new voice. It is not that women's preaching is *essentially* different, but that being practised from a different body, within particular contexts, it may become a place in which 'woman' is made new and through which women may act to change the world. And of course this is not the only thing that preaching can do, but it is a significant thing, and a good reason for encouraging women, as well as men, to be preachers.

In Thomas Troeger's book *The Parable of Ten Preachers*, the author recalls a preaching class in which the participants were asked to recall their best memory of a sermon or preacher that had a positive impact on their life, to ask why this sermon was so effective and to discern what this was telling them about finding their own voice as a preacher for the next century. A woman in the class was the first to speak. Katherine remembered going to church at a very troubled time in her life and she told them that she had not expected much more than a trip down a not very pleasant memory lane. She felt a sense of unbalance when she discovered that the preacher was a woman about her own age. The preacher spoke about the Word as the personification of Wisdom, a female expression of God. For the first time in her life she heard a sermon in which feminine pronouns were used to address God and tears welled up in her eyes. Troeger writes: 'It was as though she had returned to her childhood home to find a welcome she had not expected. No longer were the men the only center of attention. Her experience, her belief, her feelings counted as much as theirs.' (Troeger, 1992, p. 17)

Katherine's faith had been revived by the presence and speech of a different preacher. She described to the class how when she had first entered the seminar room she had noted the brass plaque on the door commemorating the women who had refurbished it. But *inside* the room there were only portraits of past seminary students who were all young white men. Katherine told the class of her hope that the church would renew itself by 'taking everything off the walls and starting again'. It was only when she had heard a woman preach, a woman who spoke of God in a different way from the male preachers of her childhood, that she understood herself at last to be on the receiving end of grace. Katherine would have recognised Carol M. Noren's words: 'When a woman who is a role model testifies to the divine, enabling grace at work in her own life and work, her successors learn to claim its sustaining power for themselves.' (Noren, 1991, p. 45)

At one of the churches where I have preached Sunday by Sunday, a woman once came to me and said, 'Now we are hearing about the women of the Bible!' I had never talked about my intention to preach differently or more consciously as a woman. And in fact I had kept to the discipline of the lectionary most weeks. But my heart leapt that something had been noticed – and that I had made a difference as a preacher who is a woman.

My grandmother is now long gone and will never know that her prophecy for my life did not come true. But I hope that she would recognise the rather mystical, lyrical and storytelling girl she once knew in the woman who now preaches. And I, who once wandered far away from my childhood delights, pleasures and longings, have found them once more as my vocation continues to be fashioned. I know I have not been anything like as radical as Katherine would have wanted. I have not taken quite everything off the walls and started again. But I have begun to preach with a voice more like my own. And not, I hope, because it matters that I find a voice to speak with which does not croak with unfamiliar sounds, but because in speaking from my own life, thought and place in the world I can touch those who listen from their place. And the more I learn of human beings and the life we share, it no longer seems so very far away.

WORKS CITED

F. Buechner, *Telling the Truth: the Gospel as Tragedy, Comedy and Fairy Tale* (New York: Harper & Row, 1977).

F. Buechner, *The Sacred Journey: a memoir of early days* (New York: Harper & Row, 1982).

W. J. Burghardt, *Preaching: the Art and the Craft* (New York: Paulist Press, 1987).

C. M. Noren, *The Woman in the Pulpit* (Nashville: Abingdon, 1991).

T. H. Troeger, *The Parable of Ten Preachers* (Nashville: Abingdon, 1992).

7

Joel Edwards

CAMPFIRE

Revd Joel Edwards is the General Director of the Evangelical Alliance UK. Joel was born in Jamaica and came to Britain at the age of eight, he is married to Carol and has two grown-up children. He is also an ordained minister of the New Testament Church of God and served as a member of its Executive Council for six years and as a local pastor for ten years. In June 2001, he was appointed as one of the first Honorary Canons of St Paul's Cathedral. He is the author of Lord, Make Us One – But Not All The Same! *(1999),* The Cradle, the Cross and the Empty Tomb *(2000), and his latest book,* Hope, Respect and Trust – Valuing These Three, *was published in September 2004.*

This was my first time at a Christian youth camp and I still have a burning image of the campfire which flooded the darkness and kept the evening chill at bay. It was somewhere around 1969 – a period filled with lots of novel experiences.

I had been a something of a church-mouse from infancy. Brought up in the spiritual womb of Black Pentecostalism, I had enjoyed the security of a vibrant and dynamic Christian faith. Sunday school, youth meetings, choirs and guitar-strumming all came with the package. It was a lot of fun and even at the age of twelve, I thought nothing of taking two buses and travelling for 90 minutes to get to a midweek church service – and then doing it all over again at the close of play. I had been a very busy church boy. I was a Christian conference, prayer meeting, Bible studies addict! As a good friend reminded me recently, I appeared to have had absolutely no interest in girls! A choice between a date and a prayer meeting was a no-brainer.

Moreover, I wasn't just going through the motions. As a teenager I evidently had an insatiable spiritual appetite. It seemed as though I couldn't get enough of church. But more important, I was always hurried along by something else: I couldn't get enough of God.

God was my equilibrium. I have no doubt about it. I wasn't any more virtuous than my counterparts and could just as easily have been lost in the moral twilight zone of the 1960s as anybody else. He held me together during my school years – I was one of only two active Christians that I knew of in a school of 1200 pupils. In a multitude of unbelieving boys, he gave me the common sense and spiritual wisdom to survive the demands of being a Christian school captain.

Unknown to me, this responsibility was a taste of things to come. For not only was I one of only two Christians I knew about, but I was also one of a small handful of Black pupils in the school. From a fairly early time I became 'culturally bilingual', meandering between Anglo and Black humour, values and worldviews. Having left Jamaica as a youngster of eight, my teenage years had become an unwitting exercise in cross-cultural awareness and survival.

As I look back over those years of exploration and discovery, it's quite clear to me that irrespective of where I was, my world-view was constantly and consistently informed by an obsession for God which drove me on through the challenges of my school-days. From the reckless innocence of an eleven-year-old, through to the diplomacy of the captain's role as a sixth-form student, I was – so to speak – a kept man.

It was somewhere towards the end of school life that the

campfire experience happened. But the story still needs a longer introduction.

About three months before the camping holiday I had the most incredible encounter with God. It still feels like a few days ago. One Saturday afternoon, as I travelled on my second bus for a music rehearsal, I was so desperate for God that I prayed the most intense prayer I have ever prayed. It went something like this: 'Lord, unless you fill me with your Spirit, I'm finished!' It was also one of the shortest prayers I have ever prayed. And then I forgot about it.

The very next morning as I strolled to Sunday school, I squinted into a blue, sunlit sky and heard myself involuntarily praying the very same prayer. I can't remember anything about the rest of the day. It was one of a thousand Sunday afternoons. But I'll never forget the night service.

It was alive. The place was electric. But in the midst of this extraordinary worship, with everyone else having a really good time, I felt like a famine in the midst of a feast. I stood by a pillar in the church and oscillated between envy, anger and hunger. And then it happened. The most amazing rush of grace swamped me, pushing aside the envy, stifling the anger and filling my hunger. I thought I would burst with a kind of joy I had never known before. I wanted to shout and run through the aisles. I opened my mouth to tell God what I thought about it and heard myself using a language I had never learned. And then came this torrent of love. Between my tears and squeaky voice, I loved everyone I saw. I even loved my mentor-cum-teacher, cum-annoying-knee-slapping youth leader, Miss McKenzie! I loved the pews and the pillar I was now holding onto. For the first and possibly the only time in my life, I inhabited a place where no one was unlovable. I loved God.

I can't remember how long the rest of the worship went on for. Time stopped for a while. But the next day at school was amazing. People were no longer intensely lovable, but the world had changed. It was as though I looked out into the playground with very different eyes. I was still the Black school captain from the Caribbean, but I was no longer as driven by a restless hunger. I felt at rest. Perhaps even a little smug, but not quite superior.

This 'infilling' had changed me and the next time I went to speak publicly I could tell the difference. So could everybody else. It would not have been my first public appearance. For as long as I could remember, I loved preaching. To this day there are three sounds which enthral and captivate me: a good saxophonist, a talented guitarist and a good preacher.

I acquired the preaching aptitude as an infant in Jamaica. I could hardly have been much more than six years old when I began presenting my own sermons as I emulated Elder Shaw. Elder Shaw was an independent Baptist preacher whose animated sermons it seemed were designed to wake me up in my mother's lap. But I imagine I didn't mind. I still have mental images of adults towering over me as I mimicked his preaching in New Town church in Kingston.

And I grew up in a tradition with a high level of intuitive training. 'Empowerment' wasn't a word anyone would use of my church experience as a teenager in London, but every Black Pentecostal church of the time had an intuitive culture in which ordinary people were enabled and allowed to develop public gifts. It ranged from the simple disciplines of learning to handle the Bible in a Sunday school class, to teaching a Sunday school class, leading the entire congregation in worship or preaching the Sunday sermon at frighteningly short notice! The results weren't always brilliant, but most of us felt useful as a result. I guess I could modestly claim to have been a regular in the local church. By the time the 'infilling' happened, most people in our church and the sister branches would have heard me reciting poetry, playing a mouth organ, strumming a guitar or shouting encouragement at them through a microphone.

But on this Sunday a totally unprecedented explosion of freedom overtook me as I stood to speak. It was a Youth Sunday and we were still in the overflow of *that* Sunday night. I was asked to speak on an archetypal Pentecostal theme about which we were all passionate and about which most of us had scant understanding: the Second Coming. I seem to recall that my small sermon was very basic. But it was also quite impacting. It wasn't so much that I had a full grasp of the text. I certainly had little ability to explore its theological nuances. But I was infused by an uncommon certainty that the story was true. My choice of words was little more than a faithful recollection of the information I had garnered from sermons and Bible classes over the years. But for the first time I felt like an eyewitness to the things I spoke about. So when I told them that Jesus said, 'I go to prepare a place for you, and if I go, I will come again…' I *really* believed it. It was as if I was there and the words of the Bible became statements to be believed.

And people believed it. It was obvious from their responses. People wept and worshipped. They heard me and believed the Bible. Hitherto people had been quite receptive and appreciative of my public efforts. Words of support or encouragement tended to come back to me. They would say nice things about my future prospects. But it had generally been about what *I* had said or done. But on this occasion it was clear that this was not about the performance: people *believed* something.

It was very moving. Very moving because I had never before uttered words which so clearly and dramatically touched people's lives, pulling them into something new which we all shared together. And it was moving because I was the same fellow they knew with the mouth organ. It wasn't a visiting preacher from HQ. It was Youth Day and it was simply me. And it was amazing because I didn't want anyone to pat me on the back. It would have felt fraudulent.

Then the summer came. I can't quite remember what motivated me to go to the summer camp. It was the second of its kind for our movement. Not everybody approved. There were a lot of adults who felt that a collection of youngsters of both sexes away from the church building was not such a safe idea. Camp was a new frontier. I was the only youngster from my church, so even arranging a lift was quite a task. I had never heard of Matlock or Derby before. In the days before multiple motorways,

Birmingham was the end of the known world.

It was a brilliant week. A whole new world of friendships. The penultimate day may have been a Thursday. But whenever it was, I remember the lights going out for the night. I lay in my bed but couldn't sleep. For no reason I could think of, fresh and unsolicited ideas were streaming through my head. The thought of a *relay system* began to take shape. I reflected on the relationship between Moses and Joshua and the pathos of Moses' unfinished business. And I thought too about the quiet patience of his assistant, Joshua, who would be the man to finish the task.

I thought about Elijah and Elisha in the book of Kings. I had never before given any time to the notion that such a powerful prophet as Elijah would have been incomplete in his mission had he not selected and nurtured Elisha as his successor. And I also thought about Paul and Timothy, the young pastor he mentored. They all had one thing in common: one followed the other to complete an unfinished task. And I thought, too, that for so many young Christians there was no sense in which they thought of themselves as leaders in the wings.

I couldn't sleep. There was no library on site – not even a decent concordance to speak of. But I emerged from my bed to catch the moonlight on the notepad I carried with my Bible. My thoughts kept flowing. It was somewhat like taking dictation. The theme I wrote was God's Relay System. I completed the outline and felt I would save it for some unspecified point in the future.

The final day was a laugh. The grand finale was to be a bonfire to round things off. But before the bonfire the planning committee arranged for a chapel service. John Francis – just a few years older than myself – was the main organiser, and as he came ambling up to me that afternoon, I knew he was about to ask me to speak in the chapel service. I could see that he was surprised when I agreed to do the short chapel talk that evening without hesitation.

The chapel service was fun too. It had a lot of entertaining items and some great singing. They called me to give a final 'exhortation' before the bonfire. But it was probably a couple of hours before we lit the bonfire.

The short address felt very much like the Second Coming talk. It had the same authoritative mood: a sort of punch into which I put no energy. I held up the stories of succession from the Bible I had noted in the moonlight. I said that although many of them had never ever really thought of themselves as successors to their current leaders, God had other plans in mind. I said that in God's long-term plans for the Church of Jesus, he would always have room for younger people and that no revolution, transformation or reformation ever took place without young people agitating and provoking change. I said that they shouldn't see themselves as spare parts but as a part of the whole; that spiritual gifts had no age limits and that all the gift of the Spirit was as available to them as it was to their spiritual parents. And I wanted them to know that the future of the Church was in their hands.

And they believed it. What followed the short address was totally new to me. People my own age opened themselves up to God. Some of them fell on their faces in worship. A number had amazing visions of God. Some of them dived for their Bibles to read things which had been drawn to their attention. Some committed their lives to Christ. The youth leaders cried and the bonfire waited.

But eventually we lit it. I loved it. It wasn't just the warmth of the fire that I enjoyed. It was the fact that as we filed out of the chapel and gathered around the bonfire, we were simply young people having a great time. It was as though we stepped out of one setting of God's presence into another. We were kids together in the chapel and now we were kids together around the bonfire. And for me, there was something in the merger of the dark and light which gave me just enough anonymity to retreat and enough light to be involved.

And I needed that space, for the events in the chapel had been overwhelming. Looking back, it occurred to me that after many years of intense hunger, God had taken me to a new place. The Second Coming sermon had taken me by surprise. But there, in my home church I was on familiar turf with people who knew me well. It was easier to think that after that initial flurry of 'anointing' I would retrieve my mouth organ and we would all get back to business as usual. But the chapel had taken me by storm. Out there in the wilds of Matlock with people I didn't know, God had done something quite public and I had the strangest idea that it was the start of something which had waited for me. On the other side of my hunger for God was a new journey I was about to begin in earnest. In the chapel, before the bonfire, a small flame had been ignited.

My pulpit journey started rather early. In my twenties, whilst at Bible College, I learned a new term: 'lay ministry'. I was involved in it from my teenage years. I imagine my involvement in the public ministry in which I was nurtured entitled me to describe myself as a preacher somewhere during my bonfire era. But it took me a long time to settle down with that title. I still remain conscious of it when I use it.

I don't think I'm proud to be humble. I'm happy to own up to having preached in some very interesting and privileged settings over the years. And I suppose as preaching goes, I can – as they say – 'hold my own'. I have known the thrill of strangers who have leapt out at me to tell me what God has done in their lives through the things I have said from the pulpit. I have also known those times when God has leapt out at me to grace my words with his presence in ways I did not expect. But I am still over-awed by this task with no journey's end.

This is because, in my view, there is something so totally demanding about the privilege of public ministry that I find it difficult to believe that I have come any closer to exhausting this journey than I did as I sat with the other kids around the bonfire. It is more than thirty years since the campfire and I still have moments in which I feel as though I have yet to reach the chapel! But that doesn't matter. It's been a great journey and I've enjoyed the trek.

8
Faith Forster

LOSS BEFORE GAIN

Co-founder of Ichthus Christian Fellowship, Faith has spent many years church-planting alongside her husband, Roger, and is currently very involved with training and mentoring younger leaders, as well as raising up a prayer ministry. On a wider front, Faith preaches and teaches nationally and internationally.

I suppose everyone remembers the first time they preach. Mine came when I was seventeen. I was being guided and mentored by the pastor of the Methodist-mission-turned-FIEC church which I joined when I made a full commitment to Jesus at the age of fourteen. Now the pastor decided to entrust me with the mid-week church meeting while he was on holiday. About forty to fifty people gathered for the Thursday evening Bible Study. My assigned passage was Philippians chapter 3, 'Knowing Him'. Looking back over the years, I am amazed to think how calm I was about it. I prepared carefully, wrote out my thoughts in longhand, prayed fervently and sought to emulate Paul as he longed to know Christ in a deeper way, and to provoke and inspire my audience to desire the same. I felt I had something to share from the Lord and I was well received by the people. In all, it was an encouraging and positive experience, and one which I would wish on everyone starting out in the preaching ministry. It was six or seven years before that first enthusiasm and confidence drained away, but that's another story.

I have always felt a deep sympathy for Moses, who started out as a young man determined to change the world and put it to rights and ended up running away from Pharaoh's wrath and spending a few years in the desert before God called him again to serve him. By then, all Moses' confidence had evaporated and he pleaded with God at the burning bush to be let off the hook (Exodus 3)!

My own burning bush came after I was married to Roger. Marriage can have a very depersonalising effect on women as they lose their name and identity and become 'the wife of ...'. In my case, it was exacerbated by being married to a brilliant young preacher and Bible teacher, who was much in demand all over the country. I felt my speaking efforts were stilted and cold (and I am sure they were) compared to the torrent of life-giving words that poured out of Roger. The consequence was that I decided that public speaking was not my gift and, with some relief, I chose to stay in the background. Of course, people were not always content to leave me there. There is frequently an assumption that the wife of a preacher must also be able to say something now and then, if only in a humble context. I was several times asked to speak at women's meetings when they were unable to find anyone to fill the calendar. Occasionally I yielded to these pressures but always regretted having done so, and finally I resolved not to be prevailed on again. My (reasonable) argument was that God had given me nothing to say and therefore it was presumptuous of me to agree to speak in his name.

The crunch came eventually. We had just begun planting Ichthus in 1974 and I was anxious to be available to the Lord for whatever service he required of me in the new season – always excepting speaking or teaching, which I refused to discuss with the Lord or anybody else. Eventually, as I felt strangely guilty about my adamance, I told the Lord that if he really wanted me to be willing to be a preacher, he needed to show me unmistakably. I told him I would accept any invitation that came my way in the next week and would give the thing one more bash. (As I had received no invitations to speak during the previous year I felt I was on safe ground.) If no invitations came in the following week, we could consider the matter settled. Guess what happened? I received not one, but two invitations in the space of a few days. The first was from a local Baptist church, inviting me to fill the pulpit morning and evening on 'Women's Sunday' in a few weeks' time. The second was from Capernwray Hall, inviting me to lead a Women's Conference at Capernwray in a few months' time! Both invitations were way above the usual run of things which I was asked to do (and regularly declined). The Baptist Sunday involved leading the service as well as preaching, and drew a congregation of about 80–100. The women's conference lasted five days in all, and involved me teaching every morning for an hour. Both engagements were well beyond my experience and capabilities, but of course I accepted them. After my 'agreement' with the Lord, I felt I had no choice.

So I did them – but I thought it would kill me! I was so nervous, I could neither eat nor sleep beforehand, but as soon as I stood up to speak, all nervousness drained away. I began to understand what the old preachers meant when they said, 'The anointing came upon me'. During the women's conference, I confided in a godly, sympathetic soul what it was costing me to minister the word of life. Her response was, 'Nevertheless, I am convinced God has called you to speak for him, and I will commit myself to pray for you to be delivered from fear, if you will commit yourself to being obedient and going forward in this ministry.' I am sure she kept her part of the bargain because it enabled me to keep mine. From that point on, a steady stream of invitations to speak in all sorts of contexts came my way.

At first, I usually delivered inspirational or devotional addresses, aimed at exhorting people to full commitment or to serve God in their own context. I had plenty of illustrations to draw from as we were heavily involved in church-planting and evangelism and I was regularly engaged in discipling people one to one, and in heading up a social action project which brought me in touch with the needs of the community and with people who had little or no contact with church. I reminded myself of General William Booth's dictum that the best preachers are those who have visited door to door and engaged with people on a personal level. This kind of 'personal work' enables the preacher to connect with human hearts, whether on the doorstep or in the pulpit. Much preaching is empty or dry because the truths being proclaimed have never been worked out in the crucible of human experience and engagement.

When I was twenty-one years old I had written in my diary that I knew God was calling me to be a pioneer. I did not then know what that would mean exactly in practice, and whether it would be in the natural or spiritual realm, but I knew it would call for costly obedience and a willingness to overcome diffidence and fear. As far as I was able, I laid my all on the altar and said, 'Here am I, Lord, send me.'

Looking back, I can see that I assumed it might mean travelling in remote areas of the world, becoming self-sufficient humanly speaking, and being prepared for loneliness as I trod a different path from others. I did not at that time imagine at all that it would involve my preaching from platforms to thousands of people, but I did understand that I was commissioned to call people out of the bondage of sin and Satan into the light and liberty of the children of God, and that it would involve spiritual warfare to a serious degree. I wrote a poem at that time which sums up my understanding of what it meant to me to respond to the calling of the Lord. If it sounds a bit heavy to you, you should know that prayer and spiritual warfare has, in fact, been a major part of my pioneering over the years, and any effectiveness on my part in seeing people turned around, transformed, healed, delivered or restored through my ministry has been due to my understanding of the need for and nature of spiritual warfare.

This is the poem I wrote at age twenty-one:

The hosts of darkness stand arrayed
about my head, and I am half-dismayed,
yet, has God said
and will He not ensure the victory mine?
If I must die I'd rather die in battle
than in the coward's cell,
I cannot see the people die
like cattle
within the mouth of hell,
and leave the powers of evil unassailed ...
If battle there must be
then I must fight
nor will I hope for victory
in just one night
(I do not underestimate the foe)
But shall I give to Him
what cost me nought
and call it sacrifice?
If I with His own life-blood have been bought
shall I pay less a price
in bringing others into liberty?

The cross is still a cross
that causes pain
It seems
there always must be loss
before a gain
(this is a rule that every soldier knows)
If in the Master's footsteps I would tread
the path is known
He was not made a Victor till He shed
blood of His own ...
Nor will the victory come to me another way ...

You can readily see I did not take my calling to serve Christ
lightly! I was outwardly a sensitive person, prone to fears and

nervousness of various kinds, so it was all the more important that my inner resolve was strong. I should point out that for me the imagery of shedding blood was not primarily of physical martyrdom (though I would most definitely have seen that as a possible price to pay in discipleship) but it was more the will-ingness to lay down one's life in sacrificial service that was in my mind when I wrote that poem. For me, the calling to be a preacher of the Gospel was not a call to be an eloquent, witty communicator, but to wage warfare in the spirit with words of truth.

In my pilgrimage over these many years since then, I can see that I have been a pioneer. I haven't trekked through any jungles or desert wastes, but I have mined new seams of spiritual life, waged warfare in the spirit, cast out demons, seen the sick healed and even a few miracles happen. I have also pioneered the way in leading and ministering for many other women, especially in the New Church stream. I was the first woman to speak from a Spring Harvest main platform (in 1984) and the first woman to speak at the Chapel Service of the Independent School my children attended (a very different experience!). I was the first woman to speak at an Ichthus congregation and celebration (and in several other New Church celebrations). The weddings and funerals I conducted in the early days were often the first where the churches concerned had welcomed a female celebrant. These things are very common now in almost every denomination, but they were ground-breaking back in the 1980s.

When I am preparing and speaking I usually keep four questions in mind to help me stay on target. They are these:

1. What is the word saying?

Whether I choose the text or passage or am assigned it, I wrestle with it till I feel God is speaking to me freshly from it. I look to find Christ in the word and to apply the word to the lives of the people I am speaking to. This might mean approaching it in a fresh way, telling the story rather than reading it, or it may be taking one phrase or sentence and hammering it home (sometimes getting people to repeat the words after me). If the Word can get into people, it will keep on working long after I have gone (home, that is!).

2. Where are the people at?

I am constantly asking the Lord (silently) that question as I begin to speak. I try to gauge the answer from the faces and body language of the people too, but that can be misleading. Most of all, I have my spiritual antennae tuned to discern where there is hostility, need, distractedness, receptivity or, horror of horrors, complacency or boredom. If the latter is present, I look for ways to break it up, to command attention. That may be through humour, silence, breaking into prayer, raising my voice or pacing into the audience. Or I may simply deal with it on a spiritual level; I have had much practice in engaging in silent prayer or warfare while outwardly continuing to speak. I bear in mind the dictum of open-air preaching – 'First, get your audience' and try to apply it to indoor congregations too.

3. Where is the Spirit working?

This is the most important question, of course, but not always easy to answer. Often I can 'feel' the engagement of the Spirit with people's hearts but not necessarily know who exactly is receiving the word. At other times I can see the Spirit moving people, perhaps to tears, perhaps to response, but just as often I see the radiant look on someone's face as the spotlight of the love of God rests on them. Whether I see anything outwardly or not I am usually listening intently to the Lord at the end as to whether a response should be called for, and if so, of what kind?

A few years ago I was visiting the USA and was invited by my host to address the mid-week Prayer Meeting. They did not usually have a 'preach' but felt this was a special occasion. Several prayer and outreach teams were being commissioned to go to various nations in Europe for the summer, so I was to address the intercessors following the commissioning. There were about 70 people present, and I chose to speak on the call of Moses at Horeb in Exodus 3. However, whilst speaking I was led to refer to the next occasion when Moses was at Horeb, in Exodus 33, when he found the people running wild as he came down from the mount of God, and in his anger he smashed the tablets of stone with the ten commandments on them. The next chapter begins with God telling Moses to take two more stone tablets and get ready to be commissioned again. As I reached this point in the story, I had an overwhelming sense that this was a special word for a particular person there. I stopped and began to speak out prophetically that there was someone present who had been a long way from God, but who, years ago, had received a call from him. They had reacted to some circumstances involving others with such anger that they had 'smashed' their calling and gone off to a desert place. Now God was calling them afresh to turn around and receive a new commissioning from him.

As I delivered this word, I was inwardly thinking, 'They are all committed intercessors here, most of them preparing to serve God in Eastern Europe. What are the chances of someone fitting this description being present?' However, during the closing prayer time, a man of about forty pushed his way to the front, pale and shaking. 'That was me you were talking about,' he blurted out. Then he followed up by telling me his story – he was only there that night because he had formed a friendship with one of the Christian women going off on mission (he was a divorcee). She had pressured him to come to see her 'prayed off', although neither of them expected there would be a preacher or speaker of any kind. The description I had given was exactly his situation – he had been bitter and angry at God because of some grievous things that had happened to him as a young man. He had not only rejected his own calling to serve God, but had become an atheist and tried to destroy the faith of others. His repentance and turn-around that night was deep and lasting. He later went into training to serve God and is involved in an evangelistic ministry today. I am so glad I was listening to the Holy Spirit that night, and did not simply follow my natural assumptions about what God wanted to do in this prayer meeting.

4. Where has the time gone?

This is a question we shouldn't have to ask ourselves if we are very structured and orderly, but many inspirational speakers derive their effectiveness from keeping spontaneity and the impulse of the moment at the heart of their preaching. This inevitably leads to a restructuring as you go along, which is not always compatible with good time-keeping. Even if the people are loving the message it is rare that a cavalier attitude to time does not seriously inconvenience the meeting convenors or mean there is no time for response or reflection at the end. Therefore, thought must be given to timing in preparation and I find it necessary to make a decision beforehand that if I divert from the prepared flow of the preach, I know what I can then omit without disrupting the harmony and efficacy of what is being said. I notice that inexperienced preachers frequently have a problem with knowing how to end, so they tend either to finish abruptly or (which is worse) to keep on adding thoughts or ideas or recaps at the end of their preach in what appears to be a desperate attempt to finish on a good note. A useful tip I picked up early in my ministry was always to write down how you intend to finish (e.g. a sentence, a quote, a poem, a prayer, an exhortation). Even if you find you don't need it, it is there to remind you that finishing well is important.

I love it when I feel I have real rapport with my audience, especially if that rapport comes from having used telling illustrations or anecdotes that relate to them personally. Sometimes, an illustration or application will just 'pop into my head' while preaching and usually this means it is in effect a 'word of knowledge' which the Holy Spirit is giving for somebody present, which makes the 'connection' even more dynamic.

I was preaching at an Ichthus carol service some years ago. During the week before, one of our housegroups had decided that instead of just delivering invitation leaflets round the doors, they would make small table decorations (with candles, fir-cones, etc.) which some of them would offer as gifts to people while the others were carol-singing. Two housegroup members went to one door with their tray of gifts while other members were grouped just outside singing carols. When a woman opened the door they greeted her with their rehearsed patter: 'Happy Christmas! We're from Ichthus Christian Fellowship and we'd like to give you a Christmas gift [offering one of the table deco-rations]. We'd also like to give you an invitation to our Carols by Candlelight service on Sunday night...' To their surprise the woman just leaned against the doorpost, saying, 'This is really weird!' She then told them she had had a dream the night before in which carol singers had come to her door and offered her a gift. When she had woken up she thought, 'Chance would be a fine thing! Carol singers ask you for money, they don't give you gifts!' Then she dismissed the dream until that night, when she opened the door to carol singers offering her a gift!

When I heard this, I told the housegroup that God was obvi-ously speaking to this woman and that we should pray she would actually come to the carol service. When I was preaching at the service I began to tell the story as an example that God can still speak to people in dreams today, just as he did to Joseph of old. As I told the story to the congregation of more than 300 people I had a sudden sense that the woman was there, so I stopped and said, 'I don't know if this lady is here tonight?' Immediately a hand was waved from the back row! I asked her publicly, 'I hope you don't mind me telling your story?' and she stood up and called back, 'No, I don't, but what does it mean?'! I began, 'I think it means that God was speaking to you and saying he wanted to give you a gift – not the trinket that the carol singers offered you but the real gift of life in his Son Jesus ...' But she immediately came back with, 'Well, how do I respond to that?'

You can imagine how the whole congregation was listening in

amazement to this conversation, and what a wonderful opportunity it gave me to divert from my prepared script and describe simply how we respond to God's call to live in Jesus. The woman prayed with me privately afterwards and became a Christian and a member of the local congregation. Such moments are dramatic and precious, though they are merely the more visible 'fruit'. Many others respond privately, sometimes not telling you until months or years later (if at all) how their life was changed by the preached word.

If I were asked what are the three most important but hidden aspects to an effective ministry, I would say they are:

1. Fasting;
2. Warfare; and
3. Pruning.

They are not things I normally share with people, but they are important for aspiring preachers to know.

Fasting

Many years ago I came across Arthur Wallis's book *God's Chosen Fast* and heard Ian Andrews speak on the necessity of fasting to bring about spiritual breakthrough. Of course, I already knew about prayer but fasting was new to me. From that time on I began to fast regularly. Usually it would be a 24-hour water-only fast once a week, but after many years I began to do it differently, seeking to engage in longer fasts of three, five or seven days. I also regularly fasted during the day if I was due to preach in the evening. Every Easter, during Lent I would engage in a 'Daniel fast' (no meat, sweets or alcohol) for three weeks or more. Eventually, health pressures made me revert to the regular but less frequent fast seasons.

During the fast I try to focus on the Lord and take time to pray and worship or just rest in him. I always end a fast feeling small, humbled and deeply grateful to God for all his loving-kindness and tender mercy. The fresh springs of life from which I have drawn usually become evident in my ministry following a fast. Something I have observed is that fasting will not bestow on you a gifting that you do not already have, but it sharpens and makes more effective the ministry God has given you. An evangelist will become more fruitful, a pastor will be more of a blessing to the flock, and so on.

Spiritual warfare

I am aware that many who read these pages will be less than comfortable with the concept of warfare. However, in Ephesians chapter 6 Paul makes it plain that if we are to be effective and persevering as Christians, let alone ministers of the Gospel, we will need to put on the armour of God because there is a war on and we are in it. You cannot hope to see men and women delivered out of the domain of darkness and into the Kingdom of God's dear Son without encountering a hostile enemy who will challenge, attack and oppose you by every foul means at his disposal. Hostility will sometimes rise against you from un-expected people and you have to remind yourself that we 'wrestle not against flesh and blood but against principalities and powers'. In prayer before a meeting you may need to pray against the hostile forces that will oppose your message; during the meeting you may need to pray silently for the scales to fall from people's eyes and for the darkness to lift; and after the meeting you may need to guard yourself against the fiery darts of the enemy as he seeks to discourage you with self-doubt or depression, or by means of conflict, jealousy or hostility from others.

I have sometimes encountered extreme hostility after speaking at a meeting, though it is often fleeting as the person allows the Holy Spirit to do his work within them. I have several times had people (demonised people, I should add) tell me that they wanted to attack me physically as I was speaking. I assure you that this is not because I have said something obviously provoca-tive or offensive but because the Spirit of God is provoking the evil spirits. I have had people fall down while I was speaking or begin to retch or manifest in some other way. Only a clear understanding of spiritual warfare helps a person to cope with such happenings.

Pruning

Finally, we don't have only the enemy to contend with, but the loving commitment of the Lord himself to our ministry. Pruning is another of the truths that we wish were not the way to fruitfulness, but inevitably it is. And it is the Lord who is at work here.

One of the aspects of spiritual life and ministry that we often overlook is that it has times and seasons built in by the Lord. Our lives and ministry need renewing regularly, not just in a superficial way but in a deep and profound way. I am talking about a form of pruning, a kind of dying even. When Jesus said that 'unless a grain of wheat falls to the ground and dies, it abides alone, but if it dies it brings forth fruit', he was talking first and foremost about his own destiny, but he was also enunciating a spiritual principle. Unless we grasp this and even embrace it, we will be beset with self-doubt and fear when the dying process kicks in.

The degree to which we experience this 'falling into the ground and dying' seems to me to be in direct proportion to the degree of our past and future fruitfulness. The mountain-top experience is preceded and followed by the desert experience. If only it were not so! When you are on the mountain-top and the glory rests upon you, and people are amazed at your authority/eloquence/spiritual power, you cannot imagine the glory fading and the subsequent coming down to earth or even lower, as God pushes you below ground. His aim, of course, is that the old husk that holds the precious life should break up and fall away, so that the inner life can push up again, just like before but with new, fresh clothing and form, ready to multiply again.

If only someone had explained this to me at the beginning of my ministry! It would have saved so many of the 'why?' questions and the inner bewilderment and even pain at times. It would also have helped me to understand and pray for others as I passed them on their way down when I was on my way up. The wonderful thing is that the process doesn't stop until we fall into the ground for the last time and await that glorious rising up at the resurrection to greet the New Day. After that, no more dying, praise God!

Until then, if you want to be used by God in a significant way, you will have to accept his pruning knife, his discipline on your life. You will need to allow the Spirit to drive you into the wilderness, to hide you by the brook, to humble you under his mighty hand so that in due season he might exalt you.

I hope this is all good news to you, dear reader! After all, you are probably reading this because you are called to be a preacher yourself. Be encouraged to continue your journey. There is no greater joy than walking in the footsteps of the one who said, 'The Spirit of the Lord is on me, because he has anointed me to preach good news to the poor. He has sent me to proclaim freedom for the prisoners and recovery of sight for the blind, to release the oppressed, to proclaim the year of the Lord's favour.'

9

Roger T. Forster

THE SPIRIT AND
THE SCRIPTURES

*Roger Forster attended St John's College, Cambridge, where he gradu-
ated in mathematics and theology. After a period in the Royal Air Force,
he worked as an itinerant evangelist until 1974 when he established the
Ichthus Christian Fellowship. Among his many responsibilities, he is
honorary vice-president of both the Evangelical Alliance and TEAR
Fund, and one of the founders of March for Jesus. Roger has written
many papers and booklets on a variety of topics. He is also the author of
several books that include* God's Strategy in Human History,
Reason, Science and Faith, Finding the Path, Christianity,
Evidence and Truth, Prayer and Trinity.*

I was slowly emerging from a deep sleep. I had either been con-
cussed all night or been given a heavy sedative; probably both. I
realised that I must be in hospital, and then suddenly remembered that I had been in a car crash the night before. The first
words of welcome in this healing establishment, in which I was
to be confined for almost three months with a broken femur, were
from the bed to my left.

'What are you then? Are you a preacher or something?' They

came from a young man who had broken three femurs (obviously not all at the same time) in his motorbike escapades.

I tried to murmur back, 'Yes, something like that.'

'I should think so,' he retorted, 'you've been preaching at me all night!'

Now this painful experience teaches us many things – sorry, I'm slipping into my moralistic didactic mode, sometimes confused with the 'pharisaic style' to which we preachers have an incurable tendency! So, back to the lesson for the day. This incident illustrates the sobering fact that from some of us who preach you don't get a decent, penetrating sermon until we've been sedated or had our consciousness violently removed!

This leads me to my only other opening gambit, which I and myriads of other preachers have used millions of times to gain attention and rapport from the not-so-willing audience – the story of the preacher who was so tedious that one of his congregation propelled a hymn book at him, which missed, striking a man in the front row who sank into unconsciousness murmuring, 'Hit me again, I can still hear him.'

The Spirit and the Word

Those of us who embark on the compelling journey of proclaiming the Good News of Jesus soon become aware that communication is not just in the trivial surface realm of imparting ideas, but comes from the depth of our being, our spirit, to the inner life of the hearer. We are ministers of the New Covenant, and so, as Paul reminds us, we are ministering not just words (although we have to use words) but the Spirit. The Spirit is as important to Christian preaching as ink is to a pen. 'You are a letter of Christ, ministered by us, written not with ink, but with the Spirit of the living God' (2 Cor. 3:3). Or again, we could say that the Spirit is as breath to the spoken word. I soon came to realise that for my life's vocation as a preacher it is as important to be filled with the Spirit, to pray in the Spirit, to exert, push out and release the Spirit, as it is to craft words and ideas. Spirit to spirit, or 'Deep calls to deep' (Psalm 42:7), is perhaps the biblical way of expressing this. So I pray before, during and after I preach that what I'm talking about will be happening in the spirit of the hearers.

It is not that words are unimportant – I personally can say without a shadow of embarrassment that I love the words of Scripture. Like the psalmist, I have often said spontaneously as I have read them, 'O how I love your law! It is my meditation all the day' (Psalm 119:97). I must have read the whole Bible through some hundred times, let alone individual, in-depth studies. I aimed in my early years of ministry to be so soaked in the Bible that I could let the pages fall open at any place, and preach from there. I used to read fourteen chapters a day, using seven coloured ribbons – five dividing the Old Testament, one for the Gospels and Acts, and one for the Epistles. In this way I was able to read, with different combinations of chapters, through the whole of the Bible, some four times a year. I also studied hard, book by book, and memorised and meditated on verses over and above my reading programme. I still think this method of making one's blood 'bibline' and one's skull 'inscripturated' is as good a way to live in the reservoir of revelation which God by his Spirit has given the preacher as is any other. If, as I believe, the Scripture is God-breathed, then it is by its very nature spirit ('spirit' and 'breath' are the same word in Hebrew and in Greek), and so must be imbibed by my spirit breathing in, by prayer, the God-breathed Scriptures.

However, a moment came when I suddenly felt the Lord warning me that he would remove my much-loved wide-margined Bible, now saturated with notes of the years of intensive study, which was like my travelling library (laptops did not then exist). Perhaps I would lose my Bible, or it would disappear in the night in the boot of some car where I'd mislaid it. Or maybe God would just take it away; I wasn't sure. But I knew I was being challenged by God.

I was being taught three things. First, that I must preach what the Lord wants me to preach, not my favourite passages, or the truths that I found easy or interesting to communicate. Secondly, I was to preach out of revelation not information. Of course, the whole of the Bible is revelation, but if I was to minister life and vision from the living God, I needed the Scriptures to be illuminated, lit up and alive to me (for me?) by the 'Spirit of wisdom and revelation in the full knowledge of Him' of which Paul speaks in Ephesians 1:17. God didn't want a 'dead' letter from me, that brought death rather than life, even if it were clever and true, 'for the letter kills, but the Spirit gives life' (2 Cor. 3:6). I would then have been like the three theological friends of Job who speak truth but inappropriately – it was truth, but it was not appropriate to Job's situation. I have had times when, alone with God and his Scriptures, the truth has been rushing into my spirit and into my mind so much that I have cried out for the Lord to stop because I can't take any more; it was even hurting.

The third lesson I was learning was that the same Spirit could reveal Christ in all the Scriptures. Jesus said, 'when he, the Spirit of truth, comes, he will guide you into all the truth … he shall glorify me; for he shall take of mine, and shall disclose it to you' (John 16:13, 14). The Spirit's mission was to show me the things of Christ. As we have seen above, Paul in Ephesians 1:17 said that the Spirit's revelation was of the full experiential knowledge of Christ. The Spirit of Christ is the one who gave the Scriptures, and these testify, or point, to Jesus ('it is these that bear witness of me', John 5:39–40). So the Spirit would reveal Jesus to me, and that was the message I was to proclaim. We are to proclaim the Word of God, in his way and in his time, and that Word, as we know, is Jesus the Son of God.

What I have explained above is what we call Christocentricism in our training programme in the fellowship of Ichthus, where I serve. It sums up the content and limits of our aspiring preachers. I confess to the students that there are times when even after all the years of studying the Bible, I wait before God feeling it is all dead to me, until something of the text lives, or relives, as it is being shown to me by the Spirit who always leads to Jesus. This, then, is the word to preach.

The life of a preacher

I knew within weeks of my conversion that I would be spending my life preaching this wonderful Jesus who had set fire to my heart and life. I wrote to an old school friend, saying I had indeed found the answer for my life and his – it was Jesus. My friend gave his life to the Lord, and spent his life translating the Scriptures into an African language that until then had no Bible. Nothing else was as important as making Christ known, even if it meant cleaning windows to pay the expenses; it was such an honour to serve the Lord.

I later read that Paul wrote, 'Woe is me if I preach not the Gospel.' Evan Roberts of the Welsh revival felt it so wonderful to know the Saviour that he would have paid God for the privilege of preaching Christ throughout Wales. I took every opportunity I could to preach indoors and outdoors: in pulpits, youth clubs, street corners, marketplaces, bus queues, chapels, house groups and hospitals – anywhere! Whatever it was that had laid hold of me, it was a calling to preach, and it drove me to make Christ known. It wasn't because I was a natural extrovert. On the contrary, I was quite shy; this was one of many things I had written down on a list, signed and given to the Lord, to overcome any natural reticence which might still stand in the way of my being of service to the Lord.

So, my life as a preacher had begun. After a few years of teaching mathematics to help pay the way for my teaching the Word of God, I found myself with so many requests for missions, Bible weekends and youth camps, that I looked to the Lord to supply my needs as I gave myself full-time to pray, prepare, preach and, of course, do the pastoral work which these things generate.

I had already begun, as I mentioned earlier, to see the absolute necessity of ministering the Spirit with and by the Word, but found no teacher or writer to expound this activity until I read and listened to T. Austin Sparks. His ministry was Christ-exalting and spiritual in its interpretation of Scripture. I had the privilege of working with him at conferences and sitting at his feet and I am glad to have this opportunity to honour this minister of Christ. He influenced Watchman Nee, who also wrote profoundly on the subject of ministering the Word. Another of my earliest mentors in Bible study was an old preacher called G. H. Lang. I didn't necessarily agree with all his views, but he made me look at the text and ask what it really said rather than what I'd like it to say, or what others' theology demanded it must say, even if my conclusion brought criticism from others. I admired the way he bore the disparagement of other preachers. I thank God for so many wonderful influences on my life and I can only hope that aspiring preachers today may be encouraged, as I was, by so many godly ministers.

Evangelistic preaching

I began evangelising in universities, sometimes taking as many as five full missions in one term. In this, John Stott was a model for many of us, not least myself, and we read everything of his we could lay our hands on. There were not so many helpful evangelistic materials for university work in those days, and John's books were assimilated and no doubt regurgitated until I thought that the material was mine. Apologies, John!

In fact, what a lot we owe each other in such matters. Have we ever said anything new? Solomon would think not (Eccles. 1:9). I often held apologetic meetings in these missions, and I thought I had wonderfully succinct answers to the problems that people have about human suffering. I trotted these out quite regularly in debates or question times. I thought if anything was purely 'Forsterian', it was my particular argument concerning suffering. Imagine my humbling shock to pick up C. S. Lewis's *The Problem of Pain* and discover the self-same argument there. I had read this book years before, immediately after my conversion. The thoughts found in it must have invaded my subconscious and regularly erupted into my preaching, letting me think that these arguments were purely my own!

Tom Rees, probably the best-known British evangelist in the

country at that time, gave me opportunities to work alongside him and learn his evangelistic style and preaching methods. During one mission, Tom's hostess fell ill, so he came to stay at my place. Imagine what I learned as a young evangelist as he woke me each day with a cup of tea and, when dressed, would have us pray through lists of people who then, one by one, through the mission, gave their lives to Christ. Prayer was the root of the power behind his evangelistic preaching. One is tempted to say that evangelistic results were proportional to prayer. One mentor told me to talk to God as much as we talk or preach to men – quite a good recipe.

Keep on keeping on

I remember once leading an evangelistic meeting at 2am; I think I had preached maybe four or five times during that 24-hour period. My fellow evangelist Major Batt was with me; he'd been a Guards officer and, soon after his discharge, found Jesus. It was said of his soul-saving ability that if he were taking a weekend house-party or a conference and three or four people didn't become Christians as he arrived at reception, it was going to be a difficult weekend!

On this occasion Bill Batt said to me, 'Roger, do you ever feel you can't preach another word more?'

I was young, and unwilling to admit to such failings but honesty prevailed, and I said, 'Yes, I do sometimes.'

'Yes,' said the Major, 'so do I. But you've still got to do it.' He said it in that clipped, commanding military voice with which you couldn't argue. Perhaps it was the voice of the Spirit? (It was this same voice with which he brought people to repentance and faith in large numbers!) John, the writer of Revelation, as an old apostle in exile, tired and badly treated, was told by God, 'You must preach again to the nations' (Rev. 10:11).

> Happy, if with my latest breath
> I might but gasp His name;

Preach Him to all, and cry in death:
'Behold, behold the Lamb!'

(Charles Wesley, 1707–88)

Personal disciplines

We are motivated by an all-compelling drive and passionate constraint to preach the glories of our God. How can we keep silent? Sometimes perhaps we must. In the same chapter of Revelation, John hears the voices of the seven thunders but is told not to communicate what he hears (Rev. 10:4). Such a restraint under the hand of our master increases the power with which we shoot his verbal arrows when we are released to speak. A preacher with no secrets and intimacies with God in private will not reach people with his sermons in public. I've tried to maintain my relationship with the Lord by a few disciplines:

1. Before rising, my first thoughts are turned to the prayer, 'Lord please fill me with your Spirit today.'
2. I try to find time to read and pray in a regular way, in the old 'quiet-time' style, as we used to call it.
3. I read a hymn every day as a love song to Jesus (especially from the old Methodist hymn book). In fact, I can't resist quoting from one of the hymns that illustrates the subject of preaching:

> Give me the faith which can remove
> And sink the mountain to a plain;
> Give me the childlike praying love,
> Which longs to build Thy house again;
> Thy love, let it my heart o'erpower,
> And all my simple soul devour.
>
> I would the precious time redeem,
> And longer live for this alone,
> To spend and to be spent for them

Who have not yet my Saviour known;
Fully on these my mission prove,
And only breathe, to breathe Thy love.

My talents, gifts, and graces, Lord,
Into Thy blessed hands receive;
And let me live to preach Thy Word,
And let me to Thy glory live;
My every sacred moment spend
In publishing the sinner's Friend.

Enlarge, inflame, and fill my heart
With boundless charity divine,
So shall I all strength exert,
And love them with a zeal like Thine,
And lead them to Thy open side,
The sheep for whom the Shepherd died.

(Charles Wesley, 1749)

4. Before preaching I ask the Lord to give me love for him and for the people whom I shall serve with his words.
5. As I go to sleep I think of Mary who will be remembered wherever the Gospel is preached because she wiped the Lord's feet with her hair. This is in case too many nice things have been said to me, especially of course about my preaching, which really belongs to the Lord. Maybe the story is connected for ever to the worldwide preaching of the Gospel for the sake of its preachers. It's a pictorial expression of Mary saying to our Lord, 'Any of my glory (see 1 Cor. 11:15) is really for serving you, and even more particularly for washing and soothing the feet of your body, the church.'

One of the saddest things I've encountered as a preacher is competition – jealousy of one another and seeking status. It would be arrogant and untrue to say I've never experienced it myself. However, since it is less than attractive when found in men and women of God, I've developed another little practice which I seek to keep alive, especially as I get older and am seriously attempting to bring on younger men and women into this most privileged of all ministries. When hearing a preacher commended or given preference over myself, especially when his theology is of a different stable from mine, I try to discipline my thoughts and tongue by finding something I can commend, and stating it publicly. I find this quickly kills the serpent, or at least puts it under my feet (Rom. 16:20). I believe the Spirit of God is pleased, because I have often experienced an unsolicited warm glow of appreciation for the person concerned as I seek to speak well of him. Surely God is pleased, who of course loves this other servant as well as he loves me?

'Do you seek great things for yourself?' (Jer. 45:5)

Compared with many evangelistic preachers, I have not often addressed large crowds. I suppose the largest crowd that I've had the blessing to address was nearly 100,000 in London's Hyde Park at the start of a March for Jesus. When I addressed 20,000 people in a sports arena in Almaty, Kazakhstan, it brought tears to my eyes to see so many gathered within a short time of Kazakhstan's separation from the Soviet Union. So many people had turned out to celebrate the Gospel and to listen to the truths of God's Word. We began worshipping at 7pm and finished at 10.30 as the sun went down, all in the open air, with some of the loveliest worship that I've ever come across. To preach Christ, to proclaim his Word in such a situation, I felt was the absolute height of human privilege – to make Christ known and bring people to the Saviour's side.

On the other hand, I am very grateful to God that I can think of some notable preachers and leaders, who came to Christ, or alternatively were called and prepared for their life's work, in some of the most inauspicious and inconspicuous meetings I have taken. The size of the meeting does not give it an importance before God. Jesus did some excellent work with

Nicodemus, recorded in John 3, in a meeting of only two. In fact it is the closeness of people to the preacher in a small meeting that keeps him relevant in his preaching to both large and small gatherings.

I have made it my practice to consider the least impressive meeting and the smallest of gatherings as equally important as larger, prestigious ones. In fact, to be true, and to keep my heart pure in its motives in preaching, I have also tried to live in line with the advice given to me by Alf Schultes. As I began preaching full-time, he said to me in his thick German accent, 'Roger, if you are asked to go to two places at the same time, go to the poorer.' I have tried to emulate that by being so heavenly-minded that I might be of some earthly good to all the men and women of all nations – preaching the Gospel to all irrespective of race, so that Matthew 24:14, 'And this gospel of the kingdom shall be preached in the whole world for the witness to all the nations, and then the end shall come', might be fulfilled and Jesus come again.

Preaching disciplines

I am sure we have all heard of the Somerset churchwarden who was asked what he thought of the new curate's preaching. He replied that he liked it, 'for when he said, "in conclusion", he do conclude, whereas when the vicar preaches, and says, "lastly", boy, does he last!'

So to conclude, here are seven disciplines that I have learned from the helpful remarks of others, even if they were not always so well meant as I have pretended they were!

1. Length
We can all preach too long. It takes disciplined preparation to preach concisely and pointedly and usually that means 'long preparation equals short preach'. It takes no preparation time at all to preach all day long. Of course, there are some cultures who feel short-changed if you stop before three hours, but this is no

excuse for missing the climax and the challenge of the Holy Spirit's timing, nor for dwindling away the power which he wished to be released because of one's own interminable repetitions, illustrations and the preacher's temptation to selfish indulgence.

2. *Speed*

When I was younger I used to preach extremely fast, and I still can if it is appropriate. I argued, with reference to the psalmist in Psalm 45, that my heart was bubbling up with a good matter as I spoke the themes concerning the King – it would pour out through the mouth as a bubbling brook. (Perhaps a deep-moving river would have been more effective, which only length of years would begin to help me create – or indeed helps anyone create.) Many would admire it, but more would lose it or not take it in at all. Of course, the preacher is not there to be admired; his words are there to lead others to the admiration of Jesus. There are moments when the Spirit's grip on the congregation mean that we can be silent for minutes in the Lord's presence and still not lose the hearers. Speed might hold attention, but it can be a substitute for the Spirit's grip.

3. *Humour*

Humour is a very common means of embellishing a message. When criticised for using it in the pulpit, Spurgeon replied that they wouldn't blame him if they only knew how much he kept back. It may be useful to gain attention, particularly from unwilling younger folk, and it may be true that hostile companies of people may be surprised by the Word of God when they laugh and are least on their guard; but I have been reprimanded by friendly colleagues and also checked by the Holy Spirit when I have indulged in this self-exalting, rather than Christ-exalting, exercise. I have repented, when prompted by the Spirit of Jesus, for being regarded as a good music hall number, rather than as a love-slave of the King of Kings.

4. *Emotion*

This is a difficult one. I believe that to love God and to love our hearers are both to be prayed for in our preparations for preaching. I have also always believed that feelings of love and worship towards our Lord are the necessary platform, or even the communication current, on which the pressure and creativity of God may flow to the hearers. To talk about eternal verities and divine compassion in boring dispassionate tones, in obscure abstractions of academia, in colourless, dry verbiage is an insult to our Saviour and beloved King. I can delight myself in some academic polemic, and draw applause from the crowd as I squash the atheist's arguments and enjoy doing it, but in no way am I pleasing the Lamb of love in whose defence I am presuming to speak. C. S. Lewis, in his poem 'The Apologist's Evening Prayer', writes:

> From all my lame defeats, and oh! much more
> From all the victories I seem to score;
> From cleverness shot forth on Thy behalf,
> At which, while angels weep, the audience laugh;
> From all my proofs of Thy divinity,
> Thou, who wouldst give no sign, deliver me.
>
> Thoughts are but coins. Let me not trust, instead
> Of Thee, their thin-worn image of Thy head.
> From all my thoughts, even from my thoughts of Thee,
> O Thou fair Silence, fall, and set me free.
> Lord of the narrow gate, and the needle's eye,
> Take from me all my trumpery lest I die.[1]

5. *Prophecy*

Of course, preaching contains many different modes of verbal communication – teaching, evangelism, exhortation, apologetics, proclamation, heralding, poetry, song and prophecy. Prophecy is a direct word of communication, from God and for God, to a given situation or person, which reveals secrets (as in 1 Cor.

14:24–25) and is distinguished by its immediacy and relevance; it often occurs while preaching, or using teaching or another mode of communication. Often I have found that the breathed word of God is given without my being aware of it; sometimes I have received it before I have begun to preach; and on rare occasions I have stopped in the flow of teaching and released what is being revealed to me as I am speaking, because I often find I am praying in the Spirit to the Lord at the same time as I am preaching.

On occasions it has been a dramatic word. That is when it needs the push of the Spirit, with a bit of faith, to overcome timidity and to stop and speak something entirely different from the subject and the flow. So to be open to God in every preach to receive and communicate prophecy is something that we need to develop – then expect God to speak. In other words, as Paul puts it in 1 Corinthians 14:1, seek to prophesy, but obviously within the context of love for God and the hearer.

6. *Content*

I have known some excellent preachers who have never spent much time with applications such as stories, anecdotes or relevant models for deep communication of theology. They say that the Spirit will apply the truth. I believe this is true, but at the same time Jesus was a master of stories and analogies or models to communicate truth; the Prodigal Son, the Good Samaritan, the 'lilies of the field' and so forth show that hard work in the applicatory world was his style. I believe it should be mine. Of course, the Bible itself is full of good material before we start, but collecting anecdotes or illustrations is a vital occupation. I used to rely on memory but now I have to write down exceptional illustrations, otherwise I forget them.

The great late-nineteenth/early-twentieth-century preacher A. T. Pierson, when questioned why people were blessed and came to his meetings, replied that he always found something positive to offer folk when preaching any part of the whole counsel of God, even including its negatives. Stories, models and positives are the hard work of a preacher's content and stock in trade. Jesus had all these.

7. Direction

What I mean by direction is: What is it that we aim at in our preaching? I'm not necessarily referring to how we should call a response, or pull in the net, or look for a commitment to the truth that we have been expounding, or even seek that the Spirit should confirm the truth within the hearer. I'm referring to the objective of our words. For many years now, I have used the words of Paul in the first few verses of 2 Timothy 4. These are in a poignant last letter to his spiritual son and colleague, and as a challenge and a test to Timothy, it is also a challenge and a test for us: 'preach the word; be ready in season and out of season; reprove, rebuke, exhort, with great patience and instruction' (4:2). Then, in v.5, 'But you, be sober in all things, endure hardship, do the work of an evangelist, fulfil your ministry.' In those three words that are used in v.2, we have a threefold test of our preaching. We are told to reprove, rebuke and exhort. Alternatively, they could be translated as to convince, convict and challenge. To reprove or convince is to present your words to the mind or the reason for conviction and understanding of truth. To rebuke or convict is to aim at the moral realm of the conscience. To exhort or challenge conveys the idea of coming alongside to help and encourage and woo the will of those who hear, into the obedience of God.

Some preaching wants to prove too much to the mind. Some forever proclaims sin to the conscience. Other preaching aims at the will to respond, with little content or reason for the basis of that response. All three aspects are important. Know your own disposition. Review your preach and adjust next time.

That's a little bit of the journey so far; no doubt there's more to come. Thank you to the publishers for the opportunity to pen these words; they have honoured me in a far more exalted fashion than I deserve. Thank you to all my mentors: I cannot tell you what I owe you all. I pray that those of my readers who aspire to proclaim the Word will be as blessed as I have been, in being part of such a glorious company of the preachers (Psalm 68:11). (I notice that the female form of the word is used in the Psalm, so I should say the glorious female company of the preachers – if I may be allowed to join such an exalted crowd!) Thank you, too, to my critics, although I won't pray that my readers will have critics; they will come anyway without prayer. Thank you, my Saviour and my God, for the riches of Christ which you have given me to proclaim to all, in your work and service, and cry in death, 'Behold, behold, the Lamb'. May this continue to be our desire.

NOTE
1. C. S. Lewis, *Poems*, ed. Walter Hooper (London: Geoffrey Bles, 1964).

10

Rob Frost

THE PREACHER AS COMMUNICATOR

Rob Frost is a storytelling preacher with an unwavering and enthusi-
astic commitment to evangelistic preaching. He presents a Sunday
morning chat show on Premier Radio, he is the author of 22 books and
he hosts a series on an international satellite TV station. Rob is the
Director of Share Jesus International, an interdenominational ministry
supported by the main denominational churches of the UK, and is also
the leader of the annual 'Easter People' Christian conference for 12,000
people. Here he tells stories of some of the most effective evangelistic
preachers in his life and in the history of Methodism. It is a challenge to
recover confidence in the act of preaching and the art of oratory, and in
Jesus Christ as the subject, object and inspiration of our preaching.

I was twenty-one years of age and had invited a group of friends
to join me on a beach mission in the Cornish surf resort of
Newquay. It was a daunting experience and I was very nervous.
On the second day, however, an elderly evangelist called Herbert
Silverwood arrived unexpectedly. I was deeply moved that this
man, nearly eighty years of age, should come to spend time with

me and the team on our first ever beach mission. He was known throughout the country as one of the most outstanding evangelists of his generation. I was even more amazed that he was willing to sleep on the floor in the church vestry! He obviously had an uncomfortable night because at breakfast the next morning he said, 'I had to get up in the night for a rest!'

It was great to have someone around who had been an evangelist for nearly fifty years, and I was constantly pumping him for tips on how to communicate well. His advice was simple but profound, and he kept repeating it. 'Tell them about Jesus,' he said. 'If you lift Jesus high, many will be drawn to him.'

Day after day I watched Herbert at work on the promenade at Newquay. Every evening hundreds gathered to hear his amazing fund of jokes and hilarious experiences, delivered in a broad Yorkshire accent. The holidaymakers loved it, and many stayed on while he went on to tell the familiar stories of Jesus in vivid detail. As he drew each meeting to a close, he would urge his audience to 'follow my Jesus, because he'll do you good!' Afterwards, he would linger to talk to everyone, from kids to octogenarians, from families to teenage hecklers. He never missed an opportunity to talk about Jesus or to speak of his love, yet it was all so spontaneous and natural. It was evident that Jesus was an integral part of Herbert's life.

Sadly, some of the preachers whom I hear in church pulpits around the country don't have Herbert's ability to 'win an audience' or to talk so easily about Jesus. They seem to have grown up in a church culture where he is rarely spoken of in a personal way. Some hardly know how to communicate the Gospel effectively to people who know nothing about him. For me, the measure of a good preacher is an ability to talk easily about Jesus in ways that make others want to know him for themselves.

Undoubtedly Herbert was a man of his time, and his particular brand of oratory might seem rather culturally inappropriate in our sophisticated society. There were two things about his style which influenced me greatly, however – his ability to 'pull a crowd' and to hold them in rapt attention, and his natural way of speaking about Jesus, which made him so real and so attractive.

Even now, over thirty years later, I often think of Herbert when I'm preparing my sermons. For, in a generation with a short attention span and an addiction to the seductive techniques of television, I am deeply aware that I need to persuade the congregation that they really do want to listen ... and in listening, to learn more about the Lord Jesus Christ. One of the young preachers I have mentored used to say, 'How can I make this sermon more Jesusy?' I found it a deeply challenging question, and as I'm poring over my own preparation I often find myself asking the same question.

I believe that the acknowledgement of Jesus as the Son of God is under greater threat than it has been for many centuries. In a multicultural and multifaith society, there is growing pressure to embrace those from other faith communities. We should welcome this kind of dialogue, but there are some tenets of our faith which are non-negotiable, and that Jesus is the Son of God is one of them. This assertion about Jesus' identity lies at the very heart of Christian faith, since only when we accept that Jesus is God and truly divine do we discover who God is and what God is like. We need preachers who are constantly asking how they can make their sermons more 'Jesusy'! Each time we speak about Jesus in this way we sow a seed, and Herbert was constantly encouraging me to 'sow the seed', even though I may never see the harvest.

One summer I went to help a friend bring in the harvest on his Yorkshire farm. I had no idea what harvesting would be like. As I learned how to drive the tractor, throw bales of straw into the barn and unclog the bailer, I began to realise just how stressful an occupation farming can be. Each night my friend and I would stagger back to the farmhouse covered in sweat and grime, but with a glow of satisfaction that 'all was safely gathered in'.

One day we had to take a trailer full of oil-seed rape from the combine harvester in the field to the large storage silo in the farmyard. I rode through the village on the back of this trailer piled high with shifting seed. I held on to the swaying trailer as we went, but gradually began to sink lower and lower into the cargo until my wellingtons and trousers were filled with the oily black seed and I couldn't move. It was not a pleasant experience! When we arrived at the farmyard, my friend lowered a large black suction pipe into the trailer and we watched as the seed was sucked up into the silo. He marvelled: 'This stuff is amazing – we sow it in pounds and reap it in tons!' Eventually I was released. As I watched the crop gradually disappearing, I remembered the parable of the mustard seed and understood the full force of its meaning for the first time. In each mustard seed of the Gospel there is incalculable potential, and its prospects for growth far exceed our capacity to understand how it happens. [Jesus said,] 'The kingdom of heaven is like a mustard seed, which a man took and planted in his field. Though it is the smallest of all your seeds, yet when it grows, it is the largest of garden plants and becomes a tree, so that the birds of the air come and perch in its branches.'

This parable really came alive for me when I visited Gwennap Pit in Cornwall. Every year, thousands of Methodists from around the world visit this amphitheatre situated miles from anywhere. It is the site where John Wesley used to preach to the Cornish tin miners in the open air, and where hundreds of them found Jesus Christ as Saviour. On one occasion I attended a service when an actor dressed as John Wesley preached in the arena. There were young Methodists from all over the world sitting in the amphitheatre. It was a powerful reminder of Wesley's preaching ministry and of the way the Lord used him to bring revival. As I gazed around at that great crowd, I was over-whelmed by the thought that the preaching of one man could result in a worldwide denomination which currently has a membership of 60 million people. It was a powerful demon-stration that the growth potential in any seed of the Gospel is greater even than that of a mustard seed!

Our approach to preaching, therefore, is different from that of a sales force for a new product or an advertising agency selling a new brand. The Gospel of Jesus Christ, when faithfully sowed, has its own growth potential. 'Success' and 'sales volume' are not primarily generated by the preacher – they are inherent in the Gospel itself. When just one life is transformed and redeemed by the power of Jesus Christ, that life has the potential to influence thousands more.

The Gospel is not some inanimate object, like a new car or a soda drink which, once purchased, quickly depreciates or is consumed. No! The Christian message has a power within it which can transform individuals, their families, their communities and their nations. Its effect and influence grow with the years. When we embark on the work of preaching, we must recognise that every seed of good news we sow has the potential within it to transform not just one life but thousands of lives. Though we sow in pounds, it will be reaped in tons.

The central task of the preacher, therefore, is to make their message 'Jesusy' – to sow this seed and to tell the story of Jesus. We must tell it in such a way that it relates to the ordinary lives of men, women and children. The challenge is to apply this story in ways that relate to people's search for meaning, and to their deep-rooted and personal felt needs. The longer I practise as a preacher, the more amazed I am at just how relevant the Jesus story is. Whatever people are facing, however they are feeling and whoever they are, there is always some aspect of it that can speak directly to them. There are hundreds of 'angles' which we can use to bring the Jesus story to contemporary men and women, and hundreds of ways in which we can introduce them to the best friend of all.

Another great influence on my preaching ministry is my father, Ronald. All through my childhood and teens I heard my dad preach most Sundays. At the height of his preaching ministry it was not unusual to see over 800 people queuing up each Sunday evening outside the Plymouth Methodist Central Hall to join in inspirational worship. But undoubtedly my dad's preaching was what drew the crowd.

My dad, now 84 and still preaching twice each Sunday, has a remarkable ability to tell stories and to make the Bible live. Deeply ingrained within me is this concept that at the heart of preaching there is storytelling. My dad would stride from one side of the platform to the other with dramatic effect. Sometimes he would shout and sometimes he would whisper. And whether the stories were straight from the Scripture or from the world of literature or the experiences of life, he had an ability to make you feel that you were actually *there* at the centre of the action.

This ability to tell stories has been much maligned in the training of preachers over recent years. Preachers seem high on concepts, good at ideas, well versed in theology ... but are singularly inept when it comes to telling stories. For me, however, it's the story that carries the message, the parable that conveys the meaning, the illustration that makes the sermon live. The gift of the orator needs to make a comeback!

This art of storytelling lies deep within the history of Methodism. As a denomination we were born out of open-air preaching meetings, and out of the ability of people like Wesley and Whitefield to communicate to a congregation reminiscent of a bunch of football hooligans. Methodist history has undoubtedly shaped my view of preaching and my view of the preacher as, essentially, a storyteller.

Open-air preaching became necessary when George Whitefield was forbidden to preach in St Mary's Church in Islington. He decided to hold an open-air meeting in a park called Moorfields. It was a rough place where crowds gathered each evening for bear-baiting, wrestling, cudgel playing and dog fights. The account of his first open-air meeting on the site reads:

> Public notice having been given ... upon coming out of the coach he found an incredible number of people assembled. Many had told him that he should never come again out of that place alive. He went in, however, between two of his friends, who, by the pressure of the crowd were soon parted entirely from him and were obliged to leave him at the

mercy of the rabble. But these, instead of hurting him, formed a lane for him and carried him along to the middle of the fields ... from whence he preached without molestation to an exceedingly great multitude. (John Gillies, *Memoirs of the life of the Reverend George Whitefield, MA*, 1771)

The meetings grew more and more popular until tens of thousands were gathering night after night to hear the preaching of this twenty-four-year-old parson. Later, the meetings were held in Kennington to provide more space, and on Sunday 6 May 1739 Whitefield wrote in his diary:

At six preached at Kennington. Such a sight I never saw before. I believe there were no less than fifty thousand people, and near four score coaches, besides great numbers of horses ... God gave me great enlargement of heart. I continued my discourse for an hour and a half, and when I returned, I was filled with such love, peace and joy that I cannot express it.

On April 2nd 1739 Wesley took over Whitefield's 'field preaching' work, and it was to become the hallmark of his ministry. 'At four in the afternoon I submitted to be more vile, and proclaimed in the highways the glad tidings of salvation, speaking from a little eminence in a ground adjoining the city to about three thousand people.'

Like Whitefield, Wesley was deeply moved by the prospect which such a ministry opened up. It gave him the opportunity to reach vast numbers of people in various parts of the country, and provided a national platform from which he could expound his message of 'salvation for all'. He was no longer confined to small 'religious societies' but had an audience numbering tens of thousands.

The field preachers of the eighteenth century were effective in reaching a secularised and unchurched culture. They were able to speak in ways that the working class found exciting and dramatic. We need to pray for a reconnection today with our present secularised and unchurched culture – a culture desperately hungry for spirituality.

There's no way that Whitefield could have held a crowd of this size and culture without an ability to tell stories, to take the people into the centre of the action and to project his message with dramatic intensity. Occasional references from journals in the late 1730s give us an idea what Whitefield's sermons were like. One day he preached to a vast crowd about an elderly, blind beggar being led by his dog on a lead and gradually edging towards the brink of a precipice. Whitefield described the scene in such graphic terms that one of the congregation, Lord Chesterfield, stood up and shouted, 'Good God! He's gone, gone!' 'No, my Lord,' answered Whitefield, 'he is not quite gone; let us hope that he may be saved.' He went on to describe the danger of trusting our own blind direction instead of trusting in the love of Jesus Christ. The sense of urgency and an ability to bring the dramatic into preaching was a hallmark of Whitefield's style.

I've been greatly influenced by my Methodist heritage of 'open-air meetings', and when I was a student at Cliff College we went by minibus to Chesterfield on Saturday mornings to practise preaching in the open air. There can be no better training for a preacher, and I sometimes wonder how some of the people who grace our pulpits Sunday by Sunday would survive if they were faced with such a challenge. The College Principal, the Revd Howard Belben, an intellectual and a true English gentleman, was deeply committed to open-air preaching. He would stand on an upturned crate and speak powerfully about his Lord – and then invite his students to do the same. I was known for my ability to shout. I'll never forget him disappearing during my oration one Saturday morning and telling me at the end of the meeting, 'Jolly good, Rob, I could hear you two streets away!'

I believe that the art of the orator with an ability to communicate by speaking simply and powerfully is making a comeback. Not on Presbyterian platforms or in cathedral pulpits, but in

West End theatres, luxurious conference suites, five-star banqueting halls, city libraries and dark smoky bars. Thousands queue for a ticket to hear Ben Elton, Billy Connolly or John Gray preach their various versions of the secular gospel on West End stages – two-hour sermons, with ice creams in the interval. Corporate executives pay upwards of £100 a ticket to hear management gurus like Charles Handy expound their latest business theories, spiced with humorous personal experiences. Retired politicians, pop stars, authors, newsreaders and sports personalities make a healthy living on the 'speaking circuit', delivering personal anecdotes over fine wine and good cigars.

In libraries and school halls up and down the UK, a new generation of public speakers are making a living by telling stories. The growth of the comedy-club circuit has been astronomic in recent years, giving a wonderful new opportunity for radical young comedians to rehearse 40-minute routines based largely on anecdotal stories. Believe it or not, 'preaching' (one person talking to a lot of other people) is popular once again.

I was once given a press ticket to hear John Gray, the author of *Men are from Mars, Women are from Venus*, deliver his theories about the sexes. About 1000 people had paid upwards of £60 to hear the 90-minute lecture. As we sat in the auditorium waiting for the start, I imagined that we'd be seeing his theories expounded in video or drama, that there would be hi-tech PowerPoint or cartoon graphics – or at the very least some interesting scenery. When the curtains opened John Gray was seated on a bar stool, surrounded by black drapes. He held the audience in rapt attention as he sold his ideas using stories, oratory, good humour and dramatic interludes in which he played all the parts himself!

The world has discovered oratory while the church seems to have lost the plot! As usual, some local churches are still in the 'Can you keep it short, please, pastor?' mode and the '*Must* we have a sermon, vicar?' syndrome. Everywhere I go, I hear that church leaders are lengthening the worship, replacing the sermon with 'discussion groups', filling the church with fancy visual aids and suggesting that preaching is inappropriate for today. The ministry of preaching is going through a lean time.

There is a feeling in some churches that the era of evangelistic preaching is dead. I have heard it said that it is inappropriate to our culture and incongruous for our time. But it's time we recognised that the evangelistic sermon is one of the most compelling means of communication known to humankind. History should remind us that God speaks through the preached word and a human heart on fire for him. I personally believe that preaching *is* a relevant method of communication and the Church should rescue it from the rubbish heap of ecclesiastical has-beens before it's too late! A good preacher's life experiences and personality are the greatest visual aids we can ever use. They will always be relevant because a preacher who has been listening to her audience carefully is actually engaging in a conversation with them, but it's just her turn to speak.

Christians need to learn the language of those who cannot understand our religious terminology. Too often we are answering questions people are not asking and speaking in ways that put them off. Sadly, many churches are so middle class in their language, dress, culture and thinking, they seem unapproachable to those from working-class or other backgrounds. And the key, I believe, is to make our sermons much more 'Jesusy'.

Recently, I was at a conference of around 70 young preachers. They were from a diverse denominational background and many of them were in their twenties. I've been hearing their pain, sensing their frustration, seeing the wasted opportunity of gifts unused. Many of them have never been affirmed by their pastor, never been given an opportunity to test their call, never had helpful sermon crits, let alone been given basic skills in the craft of evangelistic sermon-making. Many church leaders have chosen to go with the flow, let the worship speak and get trendy with the big-screen video and sound-bite messages. In so doing, they have lost the greatest means of communication God ever gave to the Church – the preacher! We have gagged the emerging generation of evangelistic preachers whom God has called for us.

The Gospel messages God is giving them go unheard, and the anointing he has poured out on them is going down the drain.

For more than a generation, the preacher has had a bad deal. He has been mocked by the media, misunderstood by the world and marginalised by the Church. There are endless courses, conferences and consultations on the role of the worship leader, but evangelistic preaching remains the Cinderella ministry of the contemporary Church. I personally believe that it's time for 'Jesusy' preaching to make a comeback.

11

Leslie Griffiths

MARKED FOR LIFE

Born and educated in Wales, Leslie Griffiths was ordained to the Methodist ministry in Haiti in January 1973. He was President of the Methodist Conference in 1994–95 and is currently Chairman of the College of Preachers. He has served on and chaired many committees in the fields of politics, education and social affairs and he received a Life Peerage in 2004. He has written five books and has been broadcasting on the BBC (including being a Thought for the Day *contributor since 1987) and local radio for two decades.*

In the beginning was the Word. So runs holy writ. And so it was in the picture painted by my memories of childhood. As I reflect on the influences that shaped me as a preacher, those sources which nourished my soul and those examples which gave me much to think about, I realised that it wasn't so much the people who performed the task of preaching that stand out. It was more a matter of the very air I breathed in those distant days. The hills were alive, if I may pervert a familiar jingle, with the sounds of preaching. All nature resonated with its cadences and all conversation was pregnant with its melodies and its eloquence.

The village where I grew up had 5000 souls. Its streets were littered with chapels. Each was crafted, with various degrees of finery, around its pulpit. Here, in English or Welsh, the mighty orators of the day would pronounce. I grew up surrounded by this phenomenon. Just occasionally, preaching could be self-regarding, self-indulgent even, but for the most part it filled our souls and our minds. We were challenged by the preacher, borne aloft on the waves of his rhetoric, caught up in his *hwyl* (a peculiarly Welsh moment where the preacher went into over-drive, his words coming in a torrent, lifting a whole congregation towards the very gates of heaven).

The chapels had their Special Meetings, their Singing Festivals, their Eisteddfods, their Annual Oratorios and concerts, their dose of visiting preachers. At school, I'd hear fellow pupils discussing the previous evening's sermon. The local newspaper carried reports of what had been said. So much of our communal life was suffused with preaching, reports of preaching, the anticipation of preaching, reflection on preaching, and a discussion of the virtues of preaching.

How could one fail to be impressed by all this? How could one be unaware?

I grew up in unusual circumstances since I came from a non-chapel-going background. I was placed in the local Sunday school by my mother, a single parent who worked six days a week in a local factory. The chapel she put me in was of the English Methodist variety, a plain building put up in the mid nineteenth century to meet the spiritual needs of migrant workers from Cornwall who'd come to work in the smelting industry of our village. The minister of our chapel lived in faraway Carmarthen. He visited only rarely. So the preachers I heard as a boy were all common folk: farmers and railwaymen, teachers and petty bank officials, employees of the local council or fishermen. They were rarely well educated but they were inevitably blessed with considerable culture. They'd read books avidly in the working men's club or attended courses under the auspices of the Workers' Education Association and could quote, in their homespun way, philosophers and theologians, statesmen and poets, as to the manner born. I never got the impression that they had learned their theology from books. They'd digested the material they dealt with. It came from somewhere deep inside them. And this factor became a very important aspect of my own preaching in due course. I grew up at the feet of preachers who had integrated their experiences and their learning within their whole being. It was very impressive. As I heard simple men and women discuss their understanding of faith and their belief in the way it should be applied in everyday life, it became clear to me that whatever preachers take into their heads as a cognitive act must somehow pass into their souls and impregnate their whole being before it rises to the surface to be shaped into the material a preacher seeks to communicate.

The preachers I listened to could all talk! They knew how to put sentences together. They knew how to build those sentences into paragraphs. They knew how to go beyond matters of mere grammar and syntax. They could always release the music of language, they could find its harmonies and its discords, they could use its energies and give shape to its potential. It was magic to listen to these lay preachers week after week in their lilting Welsh accents and, with their natural feel for style, they opened up the Scriptures and revealed the inner recesses of faith and spoke about the Lord Jesus and hinted at the nature of the Godhead with such authority that, every Sunday, I felt that a miracle had been done. It was not a matter of turning water into wine; rather it was about turning words into the Word of Life.

I've no doubt that, long before I turn my attention to named individuals I must pay tribute to a cultural matrix, a homiletic tradition, that surrounded me and infused my whole being in the tender years of my youth. The preachers I heard were still riding high on the waves caused by the Welsh Revival from the early part of the twentieth century. Its energies had not yet been dissipated. I sat under the last generation of preachers in whom the Spirit worked its wonders in this way and I well remember the Indian summer of the revival.

One incident amongst many stands out vividly in my memory and had repercussions much later in my life. I was in my mid-teens and a Baptist friend invited me to accompany him to his chapel where a famous preacher was going to be holding forth. We went and sat on the back row in a large preaching house in Llanelli. The place was packed and there was a perceptible frisson when the preacher made his appearance. He chose that evening to preach about the Good Samaritan and did so in the most graphic way I have ever heard. He turned the bench pulpit on which he was standing into the road from Jericho to Jerusalem. He walked along it as he told us about the traveller and the brigands; he plodded along in the guise of the Levite and the Priest; he glided over it triumphantly when he gave us the Good Samaritan's point of view. It was all very dramatic and greatly enhanced by the Welsh accent, the readiness to tell the story as if it had happened in one of our own valleys, and the ability to draw implications from the story without tipping over into the language of heavy moralising. It was a *tour de force* and I've never forgotten it.

Just two or three years ago I was invited to preach at Peterhouse College in Cambridge. The lectionary of the day gave me the story of the Good Samaritan. I'd preached on it so many times and, with this rather special congregation in mind, was anxious to find 'a new angle' on familiar material. I racked my brains with no success. Then I remembered the great Welsh preacher of yore. I told the college audience about my childhood memory before I proceeded to give them as near an imitation as I could of what I'd heard all those years ago. I 'hammed it up', Welsh accent and all, as I retold the old, old story. Whatever this cultured and élitist bunch of students and dons made of the homespun effort they heard that evening, I simply wanted to help them understand the strength of the story itself. I didn't want to 'sermonise'. I simply wanted to release the energy with which this remarkable parable has been invested.

When evensong was finished we all trooped to Hall for dinner. As usual on these occasions, I was asked to sit next to the Master of the College. He, as I'd learned by looking up his entry in *Who's Who*, was an expert on Solid State Chemistry – a discipline about which I knew precisely nothing. I'd swotted up a question or two in order to begin a conversation, but I was dreading the encounter. What's more, I hadn't a clue how he had responded to the sermon I'd just preached. Would he look down his nose at me as if I were a country bumpkin? Would he show disdain for someone who seemed not to have understood the gravitas required to preach in a Cambridge college? We sat down, grace was said and, before I could open my mouth, he'd thumped the table with his right hand and exclaimed: 'Jubilee Young!' I was startled. For the preacher whose sermon I'd made so much of was indeed named Jubilee Young. But how on earth did the Master of Peterhouse know that? The answer soon came. 'I was there,' he said. 'It was Zion Baptist Church in Llanelli, wasn't it?' And it was. He had been present at the same event I'd been describing. The rest of the evening was spent in reminiscing about the preachers we'd heard in our childhood. The Master hailed from the little village of Tumble, three or four miles away from my own village, and we had both been brought up breathing the same air and listening to the same theological and spiritual discourse that I've been describing.

Now that I've paid my tribute to a whole climate of preaching, a culture that seemed to endow ordinary men and women with quite extraordinary gifts of inspired utterance, and only now can I begin to look at preachers who stamped me with their influence in a more one-to-one way.

I left home in 1960 to travel the 55 miles to Cardiff where I began my life as an undergraduate. This seems a simple matter but, for me, it was a moment of radical challenge. Because of the poverty of my beginnings, I had never been away from home. I'd not had a holiday, nor had I even spent a night at a friend's house. For eighteen-and-a-half years, I'd lived every waking (and sleeping) moment in my mother's home. Everything that had equipped me for life was similarly home grown. The village was my earth and nearby Llanelli, surrounded by its constellation of villages, was my universe. So Cardiff represented inter-galactic travel! I had no clue how my culture, sense of identity, values or faith would hold up in the bracing new world I was about to enter.

I'd fully intended to put my church attendance 'on the back burner' whilst I found my feet. But things didn't go that way at all. A series of events (coincidences, providence, fate?) saw me attending the Roath Park Methodist Church on my very first Sunday and I was soon involved up to my eyebrows.

Once the church link had been maintained in this way, I began to recognise around me voices and influences that were to shape and mark me for the rest of my life. I must emphasise, once again, it wasn't so much any one gigantic figure who impressed himself upon me. It was facets of the preacher's role, insights into the differing styles which preachers came with, that cumulatively left a mark upon me. Let me try to work all this out.

First of all, the minister of the church I was now attending, the Revd Dr Ronald G Ashman, was no pulpit orator. His style was simple and his mannerisms just a little awkward. But his sincerity was patent and it was clear that he offered nothing from the pulpit that he hadn't been working with in his everyday life. Week after week he'd open the Bible and expound one of its themes. He invited us to consider what he was placing before us rather than thundering on and insisting on seeing things his way. He drew us into his argument rather than seeking to impress us with the points he wished to make. He wooed us rather than overwhelmed us. What's more, this was the first preacher I'd had the opportunity to get to know in a more regular way. We met frequently and I was invited to eat at the Manse. This personal dimension allowed me both to evaluate what I was hearing from the pulpit against the preacher's lifestyle and also to work out the relationship between preaching and the real world. I heard Ron Ashman for four years and the pastoral dimension of preaching became an important aspect for me.

Whilst in Cardiff, I had occasion to hear the pulpit oratory of the Revd Dr Maldwyn Edwards. This was a giant of a man. He was a scholar; several books on Methodist themes had flowed from his hand. He was also a social commentator since he'd worked both ecumenically and denominationally within the field of social responsibility. And he was a brilliant speaker. His words flowed, his mind seemed to encompass a range of material that he could organise as he stood in front of us, and he could move a congregation through the gears and into overdrive. He bubbled and bounced, he inspired and uplifted, he challenged and urged, he goaded and denounced, he exuded energy and joy. I got to know Maldwyn Edwards just after the year when he had been President of the Methodist Conference. He took me into his study to show me a copy of his presidential itinerary, a complicated document spread over a large dining table which chronicled his progress through Britain and other parts of the world. He was overjoyed at being able to show all this to a stripling like me. The boyishness of the man, the childlikeness of this great preacher, the total dedication to his craft – all commended themselves to me.

It was only after I left Burry Port that I began to work out just how much I'd learned from the minister there, George Lovell. As I've indicated, he lived 15 miles away in Carmarthen, so we didn't see him all that much. He came to me one day and asked me to help him. He told me that he was an engineer by background and not a particularly good writer. He knew that I was studying A-Level English and wondered whether I would correct his style in a small book he had written. I did: with a vengeance! My red pen wandered freely over his manuscript. It was an outrageous thing to do but George forgave me and we've become lifelong friends. But his genius lay in this determined attempt to challenge some of the prevailing models of ministry and to draw members of the congregation into a more responsible and participative role as they worked out the themes of their faith and strategies for running their church. This met with some resistance in sleepy Burry Port. But George was not deterred. Only later did I understand that he was beginning to wrestle intellectually with the need to develop collaborative and partici-

pative approaches towards problem solving and strategic development. He became my 'work consultant' for decades. He
deserves his mention here because he applied some of these
findings to preaching too. He helped me to see how preaching
could be a participative act. These days it's often dismissed as
outmoded because it seeks to dominate and manipulate
responses. How many times have we heard of the preacher who,
standing in his pulpit, finds himself 'six feet above contra-
diction'? The pulpit is often pilloried by people because it's used
to make absolute statements and judgements that brook no qualifications. George Lovell taught me the value of participatory
preaching, the presentation of material in a way that is accessible
to the listener, an identification of themes that are known to be
of concern to the congregation. A preacher can know that he
has the supreme privilege of working through material that his
congregation are also struggling with. They give him/her permission to do that and the whole exercise engenders questions
and discussion points and an ongoing dialogue. I owe George
Lovell a great deal in this regard.

Then there was the inimitable Brian Duckworth. I simply have
to say that it was mind-boggling to me to find a preacher who
was young both in age and in spirit and effervescent in his style
of utterance. Brian had a quicksilver mind, a capacity to read the
latest books almost before they'd come off the press. His mind
probed the questions of the day, and he was filled with a desire
to change the world. And, let me admit it, he was glamorous and
dashing and brilliant. But his abiding influence lies in the fact
that he could combine a deep knowledge of the Bible with an
acute awareness of the world around us and somehow make a
creative tension out of what might have been polar opposites.
For an undergraduate this was simply an extraordinary
phenomenon.

Then, finally from this juncture of my life, came an influence
that was felt rather than experienced. I came across the remarkable *Daily Bible Studies* of William Barclay. My sheer wonder at
Barclay's achievement has barely diminished with the passing of

the years. My shelves are littered with scholarly books. I've continued to buy and read the writings of biblical theologians and expositors and scholars of various kinds. But no one (except possibly N. T. Wright) has quite managed to distil his scholarship and offer it to a general public in quite the way William Barclay did. It was he who taught me the importance of (a) listening to the Scriptures and (b) bringing out their inner meanings in a way that would resonate in the contemporary world. Expository preaching is not so much diving into the waters of Holy Scripture *for its own sake*; it's far more to do with bringing the deepest insights that lie beneath the biblical waters to the surface where people breathe and live and have their daily being. What Barclay did in print, I recognised a preacher needs to do from the pulpit.

From this grouping of preachers I was able to identify ingredients for a cocktail that needed to be shaken in order to stir. There was scholarship and pastoral care, an awareness of the world, an exploration of participative styles, and rhetorical brilliance together with glamour and relevance. This now imposed upon me the supreme challenge. Was I myself going to be a preacher? That became a question I could not shake off.

I began preaching as a direct response to the stimuli I've been describing. I began to sense a focused need to make my own effort to share good news and announce God's Kingdom. So I candidated for the Methodist ministry and was sent to study theology in Cambridge.

I became aware that a number of people in the university were excited at the arrival of someone who commanded their respect and to some degree, their awe. Dons were talking about him at High Table and Methodists were agog at the prospect of his coming. This was a man named Whitfield Foy, a Methodist preacher with an interesting history. He'd won the Military Cross for his courage during World War II. He'd been amongst the thousands of British troops who'd been parachuted into Arnhem, where he showed extraordinary courage in what turned out to be a disastrous exercise. He showed the same courage later in his life when he preached a gospel of integration in what was then

Southern Rhodesia. The fashionable church where he'd been appointed minister soon emptied itself of most of its white members and Whitfield Foy was faced with the task of rebuilding the congregation from the ground upwards. This was work that Colin Morris was later to develop and radicalise. Morris is the first to admit that, for all the celebrity which he himself came to enjoy, it was pioneers like Foy who had traced the path that he was to follow.

Whitfield Foy returned to Cambridge in 1967, the year of my own arrival there. He'd had a previous ministry at Wesley Church, Cambridge during the 1950s and this had stirred a number of people who were to become luminaries in the Methodist firmament (at that time they'd been students in the University of Cambridge) to offer for the ministry. This was the man whom people with long Cambridge memories were getting excited about in 1967. 'Is it true?' they asked me. 'Is Whitfield Foy really back in town?'

Whitfield Foy always preached extempore. He got into the pulpit with a few desultory pieces of paper on which were written the odd quotation or reference, and poured out his soul. It was quite simply a *tour de force*. He was fearless in weaving together his understanding of the Scripture together with his analysis of the latest events in the news. His head was well stocked with literary and other materials which he seemed to be able to pull out at will. This chemistry produced its frisson of excitement Sunday after Sunday. Preaching became an event. You never quite knew what he'd say (nor, as I came to know later, did he himself always know what he was going to say). He kept his whiplash tongue somehow under control but managed to pierce otherwise dense subjects with shafts of light and probing questions that left you reeling. He was clear that the last thing he wanted to do was preach sermons to which could be added the formula QED. It wasn't the preacher's task to give tidy answers to messy questions, or to subvert the congregation's responsibility to think things through. So he stirred us alive, he disturbed our complacent thinking, he sprang at us like a fox on

unsuspecting chickens, and we all went home to talk about what
he'd said. I remember many a Sunday lunch at Wesley House
where, with varying degrees of passion, we worked and
reworked the material Whitfield Foy had put before us.

At this very same time, Wesley House had welcomed a new
Principal. He was the celebrated Luther expert, Gordon Rupp.
He'd just been appointed the first non-Anglican holder of a
University Chair of Theology (the Dixie Chair of Ecclesiastical
History) and was to stamp the previously sleepy Wesley House
with the imprint of his own sharp mind and childlike joy. He too
was a preacher *par excellence*. His style was very different from
Whitfield Foy's. He was erudite almost beyond words and yet he
devoured yards of Agatha Christie's novels and other who-
dunnits. At the time he came to us, the Bishop of Woolwich, John
A. T. Robinson, was riding the crest of a wave of celebrity in the
aftermath of the publication of *Honest to God.* It was so interesting to go to the Divinity School in Cambridge when Robinson
and Rupp were lecturing in different parts of the building.
Robinson, lecturing on 'The New Reformation', had some dozens
in attendance. Rupp, meanwhile, who was addressing the
familiar themes of the 'Old Reformation', attracted a packed
house. There was standing room only. And the extraordinary
thing was, I remember it now, that he presented his themes with
such energy and passion. He was a preacher in the lecture room.
He wanted to open his material up so that the inner dynamic
could still communicate itself across the centuries. To his mind,
the Reformation had been about the search for truth. He knew all
about its failings and shortcomings and didn't hesitate to put
them before us. But he knew too that there was something of the
Gospel that was at the very heart of the struggles which began in
Wittenburg in 1517. He was quite simply brilliant and lovable all
at the same time.

I still look back at those halcyon days in Cambridge and
recognise my great good fortune to have been there just as
Whitfield Foy and Gordon Rupp brought their considerable
powers to bear upon my consciousness, still so raw and waiting

to be formed. The mere memory evokes words from William Wordsworth that I'm more than ready to apply in a cavalier way to my own feelings at that time:

> Bliss was it in that dawn to be alive,
> But to be young was very heaven

I could say so much about what followed my time at Cambridge. And it would not be without interest as far as my experience of influential preachers goes. I lived in Haiti throughout the 1970s where I was hugely affected by simple preachers from peasant backgrounds who were in tune with the world of nature and their people's folklore. Here were men and women who preached with an easy and natural eloquence, and who fed a hungry people with a spiritual diet rooted in the real world. But I must forebear. If I were to begin on this task, my control of my material would run away from me. I must pay tribute to it in passing, however, and content myself with that. It left me with a revitalised sense of the relationship between preaching and ordinary, everyday life. And it helped me to understand that the formal qualifications and a high-falutin' education do not of necessity a preacher make. Illiterate people are not foolish people; an experience of the living God can of itself loosen a stammering tongue, fill a grateful heart and confer the gift of inspired (and inspiring) utterance.

The one single person who simply has to be mentioned before I close this essay is none other than the redoubtable Donald Soper. Like thousands of others, I had developed an admiration for his oratorical skills and became aware of his exploits both in the media and also in the open air. 'The best open-air speaker since John Wesley' was what they used to say. And I certainly concurred. I remember reading an Egyptian novel (*Beer in the Snooker Club* by Waguih Ghali) in which the writer, describing the purpose of a visit by some Egyptians to London, lists the tourist attractions that they will want to enjoy. Amongst them is a performance by Donald Soper at Hyde Park's Speakers' Corner!

During the 1980s, I became superintendent of the West London Mission and, to my delight and astonishment, found I was Donald Soper's boss! For five years I had the privilege of a very close working relationship with him. When he was ill or on holiday, I would substitute for him at Hyde Park. Sunday by Sunday I had the great privilege of hearing him preach perfectly delivered five-minute homilies on the Gospel of the Day (without a single note) at our early morning communion service. He was quite simply brilliant. There were many aspects of his speaking ability that I admired. He was not afraid to use his very rich vocabulary. I became aware that if one situates even difficult words within contexts that make them accessible to the hearer, communication, far from being impaired, is actually enhanced. Nor was he afraid of handling difficult subjects. He was completely at ease along the interface between the contemporary political and social scene on the one hand and the insights of the Bible on the other. I certainly didn't agree with everything he said! I found myself at odds with him, for example, over his pacifism and also his rather simplistic views about evangelism. His thinking about fundamentalism could sometimes also be crude. But he had no doubt, as one of Mr Wesley's preachers, that he was a disciple of Christ and that he must lay all his skills at the disposal of his Master.

Earlier in his life, Donald Soper had led the Order of Christian Witness. At the head of 'assault teams' of similarly minded people, he would invade a town or community with the Christian message. He was prepared to speak or preach anywhere. He was afraid of no audience. Whether in the House of Lords, at Hyde Park, on the *Wogan Show*, on the *Brains Trust* or *Any Questions?*, in the written press, at any old street corner, or in humble chapels and churches across the land – Donald Soper would ply his wares and perform his trade *con brio*.

It did help that he had such a fine, resonating voice. It certainly made his message attractive. But the strength of what he said lay well beyond the power of his words to compel a hearing. He'd spent his whole life addressing the social needs of our

metropolis; like his predecessors, he heard the 'bitter cry of out-
cast London'. And he knew that the Kingdom of God simply
must add value to human life; its task is to widen people's hori-
zons, destroy their prejudices, raise their sights, hold fast to them
in their darkest nights. If preaching isn't about stretching one's
awareness into these areas of human life, then its value is surely
debatable.

Donald Soper was a joy to be with during his lifetime and now,
Sunday by Sunday, I nod at the fine portrait bust we commissioned at Wesley's Chapel from sculptor Ian Walters as I make
my way from my office to the Foundery Chapel for the celebration of our early communion service. He seems still to be
keeping an eye on us all.

I baulked when I was asked to contribute this chapter about
the influences that had shaped me as a preacher. I was aware that
I had grown up in relative obscurity and long before the age
when radio and television could make or break the reputations of
public men and women in the way they do so regularly now. I
didn't think I knew people who could be singled out in the way
that those editing this book were asking. In the words of the poet
Thomas Grey, it was 'village Miltons' and 'roses born to blush
unseen and waste their fragrance on a desert air' who surrounded me as I grew and developed. And yet, having begun, I
realised just what a legacy these apparently inconsequential
people left to me. Their cumulative effect has been considerable.
Like tributaries that run into a river they've (even if unwittingly)
contributed to the flow of my own preaching. Indeed, in many
ways, they constitute that flow. My task has been to manage its
energies and allow myself to be carried away by its currents
rather than to seek to change its direction. I can only use this
essay to pay tribute to everything they represent.

12

Andy Hawthorne

JOURNEY OF A
'DANGEROUS VISION'

Andy Hawthorne was born in Manchester and rebelled as a teenager before being brought to Christ through his brother Simon. They started a fashion business and it was meeting some of the tough young people they employed that initially inspired Andy and the Message team to devise a plan to see Manchester 'well and truly blitzed' with the good news of Jesus. His band, The World Wide Message Tribe, reached hundreds of thousands of young people in the Manchester area and beyond, and also received three Dove Awards, Gospel music's most prestigious award in the USA.

In this chapter, based on an interview conducted in May 2004, Andy tells of his early influences, his approach to mentoring and his passion for evangelistic preaching.

Did the preachers you heard have an influence on your preaching?

Without a doubt. Yes. Because they were incredibly passionate about the lost and they loved the Word and those were the two things that I caught as a baby Christian.

I grew up in a conservative evangelical church that had fantastic preachers. There was a guy called James Ayre who was one of the best preachers I have ever heard, he was consistent and faithful. The whole ministry was built around this guy's dynamic personality and his preaching of the Word *par excellence*. I think that was where I caught the bug.

Also, when I first really committed my life to Christ at seventeen, my youth leader was Wallace Benn – Bishop, as he is now – then he was just called Wally. He was a guy who loved the Word, and our youth group grew in a very short space of time from a couple of dozen to a couple of hundred. We had the biggest Church of England youth group in Britain for a while there in Cheadle under Wallace Benn. We would have annual missions and we had John Allen and Nick Cuthbert and Eric Delve. I well remember as a new Christian hearing Eric Delve preach about the Second Coming and I just fully expected to walk outside and see the sky rip asunder and the Lord come back, and it was an incredible spur. I think Eric Delve, when I heard him in the late seventies, was the finest thing I've ever heard. You know, someone who was communicating truth with such fire and passion, and I remember really catching the bug, particularly as an evangelist.

What kind of a calling to preach would you say you have had?

I made a commitment to Christ when I was about twelve, but went completely off the rails and was told I was the worst pupil who had ever been to our school. [Later,] I left the school in disgrace, and was told that if I ever came back I would be trespassing. Yet within six months I was back in the school preaching. The RE teacher was so shocked – he'd heard I'd had this radical conversion – that he asked me back in. Right from recommitting my life to Christ at seventeen, I had this hunger to tell people who don't know Jesus about Jesus. God gave me an evangelist's heart, there's absolutely no doubt about it. What I love to do now most of all in the world is preach the Gospel to those who don't know it. It's funny, on Sunday somebody said, 'How do you feel about all that noise and all those kids swearing at you and all the rabble? Don't you want to just tell them to shut up?' And I think, 'No, I *love* it.' (Laughter.) That's what I love to do, you know. I've even been out there preaching with The Tribe, and there's been fights going on and snog-fests, you know – the kids treat it like a Friday night out and they're all snogging away, and you're preaching the Gospel. But there's something incredibly exciting about it and I know this is where I'm meant to be. These seeds are going to take root. So really, I'm an evangelistic preacher. That's what I love to do. There are two things I want to do: one is preach the Gospel, the other is equip the saints – that's the Church here and now – for works of service and evangelism. So everywhere I go, that's what I'm thinking of.

I remember that the first time when Wallace Benn recognised there was some sort of a gift to communicate in me, I was probably aged eighteen. We used to have a Youth Group Committee to plan our annual mission, and we had always hired these big-name preachers to do the mission for us. Somebody, one of the youth group, said, 'No, we think Andy should do it this year.' Wallace said, 'Oh, don't know about that …' and there was a bit of a discussion, then Wallace said, 'You'd better leave the room, Andy.' So I had to sit outside in the chair while a committee decided whether we were going to ask me or the Eric Delves or the Nick Cuthberts. Then the decision was made that I was going to do it.

I was very naive – I remember preaching the Gospel, age eighteen. It was the first time I'd preached to a big crowd. We had a band playing at this mission, there were 500 kids, but God did something. Some of my best friends, leaders of our church, our house group leaders in the church, the people who were wardens at our church, were saved that night in Moseley School in Cheadle. I preached the Gospel for the first time to a really large crowd and I just totally caught the bug.

You seem to preach with quite a lot of passion and energy.

I don't think I've ever not been passionate. I think Gospel preaching is more about passion than knowledge. You've got to know your stuff, but actually if you've not got a passion you've got no chance. It's a matter of the heart, a matter of the guts. Unless you *feel* this stuff, unless you *feel* people's pain, unless you feel the pain of the lost, you've got no chance. Really, the last 25 years I have been ducking and diving trying to tell as many people as I can in Manchester who don't know Jesus about Jesus, and it feels like this two-and-a-half million people is a lifetime's mission field: particularly the hardest people, the young people, the inner cities, the poor. I just feel that only if we strike *that* rock is it going to spill over and bless the whole city.

Was there anybody who paid attention to your preaching at any stage and particularly helped you?

Wallace Benn was the guy. I remember when we did Message 88 – which was the first big citywide thing I'd spoken at – sitting there backstage at the Apollo Theatre, praying with him, going through my talk line by line with Wallace and him giving input and changing things: 'Maybe say it like this, maybe put this story in there', you know. We would both go through it together.

I would preach it, then afterwards he'd pick holes in it at the end, then and there. He would always do feedback, but in an incredible spirit of encouragement. We would be going through the whole thing line by line, but he was always focusing on the stuff that was good and right and helpful. There would always be the positives and yet if he wasn't positive about some bits, you'd know they were naff. Yet you just never felt crushed by it.

Generally I have always tried to have feedback on my messages. I mean, it's a funny old thing, often straight after you preach you're not in a good place to receive the feedback, so [it's better if you] give it a few days' settling down, because your emotions – especially after a big preach – are just all over the place. How you feel seems to bear absolutely no relation to what God's done. I mean, it takes you through the mill like nothing else on earth. In preaching, particularly preaching the Gospel to the lost, if you feel you've done a bad job it is utterly crushing. I'm never as miserable as after an evangelistic preach that I don't think has gone right. I like to think I'm a happy-go-lucky guy, but I can be really down after an evangelistic preach when we haven't seen a lot of response and I feel like I've not really done it justice, you know, not done the wonderful Gospel justice. I also think you are at a low after giving out so much and Satan's in there telling you you're rubbish.

I preached at Alton Towers last weekend to 12,000 kids and – I don't think I've ever thought this in 25 years – I walked away from that preach and I thought, 'I'm not doing this any more. What I'm going to do, I'm just going to release young guys to do this, because I can't cope with this any more.' I thought, 'That's it, I'm stuffing preaching now.' I wasn't thinking, 'I'm going to give up being a Christian.' I'm definitely thinking, 'I'm giving up preaching.' I just thought I'd not done a good job and I drove home really depressed, actually, really down. Then I got three text messages on my phone, quickly, right after each other: 'My friend's just become a Christian …' 'That was amazing, that …' You know, just three absolute peaches. One from one of our Eden Team saying there's an out-of-control girl who's just committed her life to Christ and she's just 'got' the Cross, and I thought two things. I thought, 'God's good, the Body of Christ's good.' But I also thought, 'How easy was that for those people!' It took them about ten seconds, especially at the speed that our lot do text, but what a blessing it was to me. Just that little encouragement – that they didn't need to do – totally changed it for me.

Do you have any mentors or coaches right now?

I try to make myself accountable to some really great men of God. I meet regularly with Rob Munro, who's the minister of my church, and with Rob White, who is the minister of Poynton Baptist Church and one of our Trustees, and I try to meet those guys once a month. And I also meet now with a group of seven young evangelists who are part of the Message to try to sharpen them and to encourage them, and we criticise each other's messages, etc. And I try to give them bigger and bigger platforms.

How do you go about training and developing young preachers in the Message?

There are about 60 people who work full-time for the Message and perhaps seven of them have special gifting and anointing for preaching the Gospel. Part of the problem is that we think as soon as anybody is a keen Christian they've got to preach, and so we put all sorts of people who are hopeless communicators up there preaching.

I would say the worst possible track for learning to communicate the love of Christ successfully from a platform is: public school – university – Bible college – church. I would think that would be how *not* to get somebody able to connect with ordinary people. You could not get a worse model, if you ask me. So we just need to get people out into the real world. The number one best-selling newspaper is the *Sun*. The number one watched programme is *Eastenders* or *Coronation Street*. Our trouble is that we live in a completely different stratosphere in terms of the way we try to communicate to people.

What qualities do you look for in young preachers you are bringing on?

First, there's the supernatural fruit that they bear. Because with real preaching in the power of the Spirit you will see the fruit. There will be different quantities and different qualities of fruit, and I am never going to bear the same fruit as Billy Graham. You are going to see fruit, however. There's going to be a real evidence of life breaking out when you share the Gospel and you preach the Word – things are going to happen.

The second thing is, there's that heart. One of my touchstone verses is: 'The eyes of the Lord range the earth looking for a heart fully after him; this man he will strongly support' (2 Chronicles 16:9). The Lord is looking, he's constantly looking for that heart, looking for someone who will delight themselves in him and then he will give them the desires of their heart. You know that verse, 'Delight yourself in the Lord and he will give you your desires.' We've made it a man-centred verse. It's not a man-centred verse at all, it's a God-centred verse. It's 'Delight yourself in the Lord and he will give you the desires of your heart.' In other words, you will find your heart desires for the poor to be touched, for the marginalised to be reached, for the lost to find Christ. You'll find it's God-type desires that you have now, and you will find it's as opposite to a prosperity Gospel as you can get.

I think the Lord is looking for some of that gutsy heart and the first thing you want to see is that determination, that passion for the lost, passion for the Kingdom. Then obviously you look for fruit, and finally a natural ability that can be fanned into flame.

So are you a natural public speaker?

I am a bit of a showman, without a doubt. I think I was always the clown at school, always the one trying to be the centre of attention; then I became a salesman and I was a pretty good salesman, which often goes with that whole thing, that whole natural ability to communicate. I've preached to some pretty big crowds and I'll really find that exciting and challenging, but wherever I go I like to think I'm a raconteur, telling stories, and I am naturally extrovert. I am naturally more a feeler for the people, so while I enjoy having my head buried in my studies, reading books, actually I am energised by people.

How do you think the WWMT and the Message Trust have helped you develop as a preacher? [1]

A lot goes back to Message 88, that my friend Mark (Pennells) set up, wanting to do this schools ministry called 'Message to Schools' and he asked if I would help him do this schools work. I was so taken by it that I ended up spending half my time on it, pulling out of the business, that I was running with my brother, and doing the lessons and assemblies with him. We set up this little trust called Message to Schools to employ Mark. I will never forget the first schools mission we did, in Woods Lane High School in Cheadle Hulme and in a massive hall. We had done lessons and assemblies during the week and on the Friday night Mark did his songs, and there were 75 bored teenagers round the side of this thing. And then I got up to preach, and preached my heart out, did my best and I said to them, 'If you really feel like you want to respond to what you have heard this week and tonight, myself and Mark are going into the gym next door and if you'd like to come in and pray with us and give your life to Christ, go next door.' We went next door and 37 kids came through out of the hall, and just watching them I felt God had done something. There was real hunger there, real desire. We led all these kids to the Lord and it was really amazing.

Something started then and I do think the eyes of the Lord ranged the earth, and saw something in myself and Mark, a heart for mission, for the lost. And God just gave me bigger and bigger platforms because, y'know, shortly after that I started doing this funny rapping with Mark to set up my preach. I'm not a singer/dancer/rapper, y'know, I can't play the instruments, but we found that by doing this music together; me rapping, Mark singing and doing this dance music, suddenly we didn't have 75 kids, but 7500. It just blew up and I had this massive platform and I kept thinking, 'What a fraud I am!' I'm doing this rapping, sounded like a demonised member of Sesame Street. Have you ever heard the early World Wide Message Tribe? You didn't miss anything. But the kids absolutely went mad for it, and I just had this platform for preaching that I couldn't have dreamed. I have preached at all these football stadiums, great arenas, but God just opened all these doors. It was really amazing and I've always said, ever since, to the Tribe (the band has been through various stages, various line-ups), and I've always said to the guys, 'First and foremost you're Bible teachers. If you don't spend more time Bible teaching than you do singing and dancing and rapping, you've lost the plot. You're gonna do that in all sorts of wacky, creative ways. We're gonna push the boat out, but the ultimate objective is to get the Word of God out to these young people, because there's power there.'

A lot of my preaching still to scally teenagers is kind of expository, really – verse, verse, verse, etc. But I'm thinking, how do we communicate that into MTV culture?

Can you talk about the church or theology that has had the biggest impact on your preaching?

The Soul Survivor grouping has had a big impact on me, for good. Coming from my background of conservative evangelical, I was really committed to the Word, wanting to preach the Word, but open to the Holy Spirit, gently charismatic. What really impacted on me was the way they were able to do the response, look for response to the preaching, without it being wacky and whipped up and just letting God do his thing, basically. That's been a real eye-opener to just watch God. I don't know whether you know Mike Pilavachi at all, but his ministry style is amazing. It is not whipping up 'God, come, come, come!' It's just 'Let's just see what God wants to do, just chill out.' He'll often tell a joke, he almost always tells a joke so that 'this isn't me whipping it up, this is God coming down', y'know. It's been a real eye-opener to see God do stuff at Soul Survivor.

There is an expectancy there. The key thing is faith, isn't it? There's an expectancy, you know. The preacher, as far as I can see, needs to have various things. There's the need to *understand the passage,* you also need to have *clarity,* and you need to have *faith*:

faith to believe that there will be a response to what you've said. There's an expectant faith and without those things you are stuffed, you are not going to see God do his thing. That faith bit is the fascinating bit.

And do you have particular preachers you look up to?

Billy Graham, the great hero of any preacher, is somebody who is here on my wall. My one purpose in life is to help people find a personal relationship with God, which I believe comes with knowing Christ, which this quote from Billy Graham expresses: 'I will never do anything as long as I live except preach the Gospel and I intend to do that as long as God gives me breath.'

I well remember the first time I heard Billy Graham, live. I'd booked all these coaches to take people from Cheadle to Anfield and the sense of expectancy as you go and hear the great man … the football stadium's full and then he gets up to preach and, to be honest, it was so disappointing. You are just thinking this is the greatest communicator you have ever heard in the history of the world and … it's just a string of scriptures strung together with a few stories, not very well told jokes and, y'know, at the end of it he says, 'And now thousands of you are going to come forward and give your life to Christ.' And you think, 'Oh, yeah, sure thing, Billy!' and sure enough, thousands of them, including my mother-in-law who was sat next to me, and it was just an amazing thing and the key is just seeing, over and over and over again, that the Gospel does its work. As long as the preacher is faithful.

Can you tell me anything about the pain or difficulties you have faced as a preacher?

I remember Message 89. Preaching the Gospel to 3000 kids in the evening, and in the morning the business I had with my brother Simon had gone into liquidation. We had this great surge in turnover making braces, and then braces had gone out of fashion and we had all these million yards of elastic in stock and all this machinery and all this debt, and we just got into terrible trouble, and we were spending all our time doing the Message, instead of running the business. It was a horrible day really. In the morning I was signing the business away to the liquidators and in the evening I was preaching the Gospel, and it's like sometimes that stuff happens. We were trying our best at that point in our lives, trying our best to make Jesus known and we were seeing some amazing fruit. God was doing this new thing in Manchester and yet financially for us it was a disaster. It was an absolute mess. Sleepless nights and all that. Sometimes those things go together, don't they? Sometimes horrible things happen just when you are right, trying to do the best you possibly can.

I tell you what it taught me. A lot of preaching is getting on with it, through thick and thin. It's gutsily being faithful, and sometimes it is gritting your teeth. The life of a preacher is just not easy.

The problem with heading up a ministry like the Message, fast-growing and dynamic though it is, is the hassle. It's sheer hassle and aggravation and sometimes it's all you can do to keep going. It just takes determination and plodding because there's sometimes personal hassle and sometimes financial pressure that you just wouldn't believe. A little story comes to mind that might be relevant. Somehow I have got on George Verwer's prayer list. Do you know George Verwer? He has this unbelievable prayer list, I don't know how many people he must pray for. But once every six months, I get this call. It's always just at the right time, when I'm feeling down. He just phones up: 'How you doing, brother, y'okay? I'm for you. I'm going to send you a few pounds because I believe in you ...' and all this.

About a month ago, he phoned me up and I was really down and we couldn't pay the salaries, we couldn't pay some bills. He said, 'How you doing, brother?' I said, 'I'm struggling, to be honest, George. It's really hard work and it just feels like I'm just not getting there.' And he rose to this challenge like a man possessed, actually, possessed by the Lord of course. (Laughter.)

He was shouting down the phone, 'Don't you dare give up, brother! If I can do this for 45 years through financial challenges and battling with lust ... I've had my team let me down and I've had people rip me off for a million dollars ...' Well, I've got the phone held out here and he's shouting at me, and I felt it was like, 'I've run the race, I've fought the fight, and you flipping get on with it. Just keep on going, boy!' It was so good for me.

Finally, I remember hearing about Billy Graham coming over to England in the fifties for Harringay and nobody wanted to know him and all the press were slaughtering him. And he was just kneeling on the bedroom floor in his little bedsit before he went out with Ruth, saying, 'Lord, what is going on?' And of course the rest is history. We see the history, but we don't see all the pain that goes into the whole business.

NOTE

1. For a fuller story see Andy Hawthorne, *Diary of a Dangerous Vision* (London: Kingsway, 2004).

13

Anthony Reddie

AN INTERACTIVE
ODYSSEY

Dr Anthony Reddie is a Research Fellow and Consultant in Black Theological Studies for the Queens Foundation and the Methodist Church. He has written a number of books in the areas of Christian education and Black theology. His latest book is entitled Acting in Solidarity: Reflections in Critical Christianity *(2005). He is also the editor of* Black Theology: An International Journal.

The raw material for the budding preacher

I am an African Caribbean Black male in his forty-second year. I was born into and have been socialised within a Caribbean home of Jamaican migrants to Britain. I have chosen to give you these bare facts by way of an introduction because to understand my approach, commitment to and, dare one say, sheer enjoyment of preaching, one needs to understand something of the context into which I was nurtured.

Growing up in a Caribbean household was a fascinating experience. The world that was inhabited by my parents was one that was separated from the wider arena of White working class life in Bradford, West Yorkshire. My parents, in order to shield themselves and their children from the ongoing shadow of racism that seemed to stalk the lives of Black migrants living in Yorkshire, constructed an elaborate internal universe of ritual, belonging and, best of all, storytelling that was to be our bulwark against the harshness of the outside world.

In this self-enclosed world, living in the back room of our terraced house, that also served as a dining room and a kitchen, my parents told of a magical world that was back home in the Caribbean. It was a world punctuated by seemingly exotic creatures and extravagant, idiosyncratic characters. This was a world that captured my imagination and that of my three siblings.

The best of times in the relatively small, close-knit community of African Caribbean migrants in Bradford were those moments when members of the extended family and other close friends would visit our home and, over the course of several hours, myriad stories would ensue, each told with panache and liberal amounts of jocularity. It seemed like a magical time. In many respects it was.

What I took from this world of storytelling and colourful narratives was the importance of being able to tell a story and hold the attention of an expectant audience. The great champion storytellers were my mother and my Auntie 'Dotty',* my mother's only surviving sister. These two individuals were the special women in my early life, and they were very different. My aunt was strident, ebullient and headstrong, whereas my mother was more quiet, reflective and circumspect; but both of them were united by an amazing ability to tell a good story.

Witnessing the elders in my family and wider community waxing lyrical as they told stories from the dim and distant past and those of a more recent vintage, I learned one of the central

* It is not uncommon for many Caribbean people to be given 'pet names', which become the popular means of identification of the person, often-times in preference to their given 'Christian' names.

truths of 'good preaching' – namely, that good preaching paints vivid pictures and images in the mind of the listener. The power of inspired oratory transports the listener to 'another space and time'. When the elders in my family were regaling their younger charges with dramatic stories of 'back home' (in the Caribbean), it often felt like you were there whilst the narrative was unfolding.

Given the age stratification in this cultural environment, children were mostly invisible, in that they were rarely seen and certainly not heard. This cultural and community-orientated event was most definitely an adult affair. Whilst I was rarely permitted to share any of my stories in these settings (as a child, I doubt I had a great pool of experience on which to draw in order to tell an entertaining tale, anyway), I did learn how to tell a story.

As the elders congregated in the 'front room' and we younger folk were banished to the more mundane climes of the back room, my siblings and I would occasionally peek our heads around the door in order to get a glimpse of the adults at play. Peering through the gap in the slightly opened door I saw my parents and their peers laughing, joking and expressing their exuberant and defiantly hopeful selves in a manner that so rarely found expression in their more public identities in the wider society of Bradford. People who so often were repressed and diminished by the forces of racism and struggle were, in this particular setting, wonderfully expressive and unself-conscious entertainers.

Putting on the style

One of the most important lessons I learned about Black story-telling was that style was as important as content. It was not just a question of what you said, although, as I will demonstrate at a later juncture in this chapter, that is of crucial import; it was also a matter of how it was said. A central truth of all good story-telling is its discursive qualities. Narratives never come alive when they are expressed in a kind of objective, dispassionate, report-writing form, or technical framework. I am sure we have all sat through the kind of 'And then I did this, and then this happened, and then that happened' kind of utterance. Simply telling the 'facts' as we understand them rarely makes for riveting storytelling. Jesus was a storyteller *par excellence*! The power of the Gospel is the power of a captivating narrative.[1]

An essential piece of learning that emerged from those many occasions watching my familial and community elders resplendent in their storytelling practices was the sense that context was everything. The best narratives came alive when the storyteller was able to embellish the bare facts with a plethora of asides, carefully crafted segues and other forms of extraneous information; all of which upon first hearing might appear superfluous, but upon further reflection proved themselves to be utterly indispensable.

I was struck by the unerring ability of my Auntie Dotty or one of my uncles to take a quick detour from the main thread of the narrative, in order to incorporate some scatological comment on a present-day happening in the city or the country, throw in a few other comments for good measure, and then return to the central thread of the story without appearing to miss a beat. This was exhilarating stuff. At a later point in this chapter, I will talk about jazz music as a means of constructing a theoretical framework for a Black theological and discursive approach to narrative and preaching: but more of that in a moment.

Connecting with good Doctor Bill

The church into which I was socialised, and in which I learned a good deal of what it meant to be a Christian, was called Eastbrook Hall. Eastbrook was the central Methodist Mission in Bradford. It was a large, ornate building. My family decamped to Eastbrook when Prospect Hall Methodist church, in which I had been christened, was closed in the late 1960s. The earliest superintendent minister I can remember at Eastbrook was the Revd

George S. Beck, but the one who made the biggest impact upon my budding, pre-public emergence as a preacher was the Revd Dr William R. Davies.

As members of the Youth Fellowship at Eastbrook, we would attend evening worship on a Sunday (which was the principle service for the day, not the morning one) prior to meeting as a youth group after worship. The group would sit high in the stratosphere, in the balcony, to the left and slightly behind the preacher. From this vantage point, one could see the preacher 'do his stuff'. I never got to preach at Eastbrook. But sitting in the balcony with the angels, one got to see at first hand how a preacher could bestride the acres of space that was the pulpit and declaim the Gospel to all and sundry from a vantage-point that was perched way up in the sky, far removed from the massed ranks of humanity on the ground (save for those in the balcony, that is).

Memory can be a fickle mistress, but from what I remember, the preaching of Dr Bill Davies was undertaken without notes. He wore a pin microphone and would go 'walk-about' across the pulpit as he seemed to pluck one random thought from the air after another, stringing these thoughts together with an elo-quence and a beauty that left me awestruck. 'This man is good' I thought to myself. Bill Davies seemed for all the world to be making it up as he went along. His formidable scholarship was kept closely out of sight, as a torrent of stories, anecdotes, dramatic pauses and casual asides brought the Gospel to life.

It was never my intention to consciously seek to emulate Dr William R. Davies, and the truth is, our respective theologies are very different and my own preaching ministry is quite different also. But what I learned from Dr Davies was the theatre of preaching. Good preaching is theatre!

The development of the public preacher

I preached my first sermon whilst on a Birmingham University Methodist Society (Meth. Soc.) Easter mission in the Black

Country in the mid-1980s. I cannot remember much about the
sermon, save for the fact that it was short, utterly trite and
wonderfully naive in its assumptions about the people who
might be on the receiving end of it. The underlying 'problem'
with the early years of my preaching ministry was the lack of
awareness of the contextual or cultural elements in my life which
could and should have served as a basic foundation for proclaiming the Gospel. All the aforementioned factors, arising from my
upbringing, such as my parents' narrative skills or incorporation
of Scripture into the very fabric of the mundane and the ordinary,
all these factors were sadly missing in my preaching.

The subconscious influences of Black cultural life that I had
imbibed from my parents and my wider family had failed to find
a home within my conscious calling and practice as a Methodist
Local Preacher. I was unable to reconcile the generic perceptions
of being a preacher, which I gained from being on the approved
national training course for the development of preachers,[2] with
the more specific skills I had learned from my parents, neither of
whom (at that time) were called to preach. My preaching was
largely formulaic and lacking in any distinctiveness as a result of
my trying to become a 'good White middle-class Methodist Local
Preacher'. My preaching was nondescript because I was denying
my formative roots and the compelling narrative strength that is
Black orality.

Discovering my voice – an interactive approach to preaching

The turning point for me in my development as a preacher
occurred when I commenced my research for my doctorate. My
research, funded largely by the Methodist Church, but supported
by the Anglican and United Reformed Churches, was concerned
with the nurture and empowerment of Black children and young
people, their families and the wider community, by means of the
Gospel of Christ. My task was to find more culturally appropriate ways of sharing Christianity with Black people in order that

the faith might come alive and become an empowering and affirming resource for their lives.[3]

One of the expectations of the field officer appointed to this project was that they would speak to (often a carefully crafted synonym for people to preach who are not authorised to do so) and engage with inner-city, multiethnic churches in Birmingham. One of the tasks of these 'talks' (often in morning worship) was to enable the largely White leadership in the form of preachers (lay and ordained) and children's and youth workers to understand the necessity of engaging with Black popular culture in order that the Gospel might reflect and respond to issues that have arisen out of the Black experience.

It became apparent, very quickly, that many of the older White people holding office and who exerted a strong measure of power and influence in these inner-city churches were not going to be swayed by a young Black upstart lecturing, hectoring and talking at them. I learned that it was imperative that I find a way of engaging with them – i.e. trying to win them over and get them on my side.

My preaching style began to emerge

The breakthrough in my development as a preacher occurred one Sunday morning in mid-1995. I was invited to speak at a multiethnic inner-city Anglican church in Birmingham. I had been invited by the incumbent to talk about my developing research and how the church might contribute to the project. I thought about how I might engage the congregation in the 15 or so minutes I had at my disposal. How could I help them to understand the need to reinterpret the Gospel in light of the Black experience?

Whilst I was in the process of contemplating how I might make the most of this opportunity I was immersed in reading about the work of Thomas Groome. Groome has been a major proponent of an interactive, participative approach to practical theology. He argues that activity and joint participation are

central to the teaching and learning process of Christian education.[4] In a later work, he develops further his notion of Christian
reflection which gives rise to committed action in the name of the
Gospel (often termed *praxis*), and constructs an overarching
concept for a radical approach to practical theology.[5] In this
seminal work, he outlines an approach he calls 'Shared Praxis',
which he describes as being 'a participative and dialogical
pedagogy in which people reflect critically on their own historical agency in time and place and on their socio-cultural reality,
have access together to Christian story/vision and personally
appropriate it in community with the creative intent of renewed
praxis in Christian faith towards God's reign for all creation'.[6]

Groome details an approach that attempts to link the individual to a process of critical reflection and dialogue. This reflection
and dialogue arises through a shared process where individuals
are encouraged to enter into dramatic exercises that attempt to
address major issues and concerns in the lives of that group of
people. This dramatic exercise is, in turn, combined with the
sacred stories (or narratives),[7] in order that the Christian
story/vision, namely the Gospel of Christ, can be realised.

This process culminates in the final phase of this approach,
which is a search for the truth that enables participants to make
the Christian story their own.[8] Groome argues that participants
should be empowered to appropriate the story/vision in order
that they can own it, and then remake it, so that they can be set
free. Groome's approach is heavily influenced by Liberation
theology and seeks to speak to the experiences of those who have
been marginalised and oppressed.

Once I had discovered this theory, I wanted to see if there was
a way I could use it within a 'sermon slot' in order to raise a
number of important theological and educational points concerning my research. In short, could this technique 'win over' the
folk in this church? The theme for the service at this particular
Anglican church was 'God's Story, Our Story and My Story' and
was an invitation to look at how the Gospel of Christ connects
with us, from the individual to the corporate and, ultimately, to

the very source of all that is, through the transformative work of Christ.

In order to support and empower the congregation to catch hold of this idea and its relationship to marginalised and disempowered Black children and young people and their families, I created a participatory exercise for the whole congregation. In this exercise, I wanted to demonstrate how a Eurocentric interpretation of Christianity had led many Black people to reject the Christian faith on the grounds that it was a religion of exploitation, created for White people by White people.

The exercise I created was entitled 'Are You in the Story?'. After further revisions and amendments it was later incorporated into the introductory material in Volume 2 of *Growing into Hope*.[9] This exercise was intended to help leaders understand more clearly a process that has afflicted African people for approximately five hundred years. A process of miseducation and biased, self-serving teaching strategies have led African people to develop a negative psychological condition manifested primarily as a form of self-denial. This can be seen in the inability of 'colonised' people to assert their own worth, or to see themselves reflected positively in popular stories, myths or historical events.

The aim of this training exercise is to describe clearly one of the principal sub-texts of *Growing into Hope*, namely, the need for oppressed people to use the story/vision (of the Gospel) for their ultimate liberation. This work enables Black youth (in fact, all marginalised peoples) to claim the Gospel of Jesus Christ as their own.

The exercise asks individuals to imagine a scene from the Bible – I chose John's account of the 'Feeding of the five thousand' in chapter 6, verses 1–15. All participants are asked to imagine the scene in the story in as much detail as is possible. What does Jesus look like? What are the disciples like? What is the boy wearing? How do they see the crowd? Having imagined the scene in great detail, individuals are then asked to reflect upon where they are in the story. If individuals see themselves as one of the disciples at the centre of the story, then they are encouraged to walk to one particular side of the room. Conversely, if they are mere bystanders, near the back of the crowd, then they are encouraged to walk to another side of the room. Finally, I ask if any are even in the scene at all, or whether they are watching the action as if they are in a living room, far removed from the whole event, viewing everything on television.

The crucial learning that resulted from this exercise was the sense that marginalised and oppressed Black people tend to see themselves as distant spectators in God's story, not as central players.[10] This in itself should not surprise us. If broader society largely confines Black people to subservient and demeaning roles, then why should we necessarily expect these selfsame people to imagine themselves in central, defining positions within biblical narratives?

As I have stated elsewhere, such is the reinforced hierarchy in the Church, which simply replicates the practices of broader society, that if you are a 'somebody' in the world, then you will be a 'somebody' in the Church. Conversely, if you are a 'nobody' in the world, then you will be as much a 'nobody' in the Church. The theology of the inverted Kingdom where the first are last and the last are first, is really nothing more than pious rhetoric in many of our churches.[11]

This exercise was created in order to bring to life a central idea of Groome's: namely, the notion of inculturation – the expression of the Gospel through a specific culture (located in a specific period of time). This process includes the appropriate resetting of the sacred narrative, bringing the story to life and localising the story/vision.[12] On this subject Groome writes: 'Christian faith is expressed in people's lives through symbols and modes native to their culture. It is a source of transformation for the cultural context – each cultural expression of it renews and enriches the universal Christian community.'[13]

In using this exercise, I was able to challenge this church to think about the images, symbols and cultural contexts in which the Christian faith was both expressed and imagined. I impressed upon them the need for people to be empowered to imagine themselves and their accompanying cultures at the centre of the Gospel narrative, in ways which counteracted the often marginalised and humiliating status imposed upon them in the wider society.

Living with vulnerability

As I have been recounting this story, I have had a sense of the anxiety and the tension that polluted my mind and body as I walked that morning towards this Anglican church ready to unleash this crazy exercise on an unsuspecting and polite Sunday morning congregation. What was scary about the whole venture was the realisation that I could not foresee or guarantee the reaction of the congregation. What if they refused to 'play along with me'? What if my mirth-making and 'tomfoolery' offended their polite Anglican sensibilities?

The truth is, what scared me the most was the realisation that I could not script an interactive activity. Yes, I could make notes and gear myself for a possible range of responses; but ultimately, there was no certainty as to what response would ensue and how I would handle it. I was scared to death, but determined to carry it through.

The most remarkable piece of learning that emerged from that poignant moment in 1995 was the sense that I had reconnected with my formative roots within the Black African/Caribbean tradition. African and Caribbean people are oral people. We love storytelling and interaction.[14] Standing in the glare of a large multiethnic congregation, my fear disappeared. All the comedic and performance skills I had witnessed in my parents, and which had lain dormant in me for many years, suddenly came to life. I revelled in the seemingly unstructured nature of it all. My brain was running at a hundred miles an hour, always three steps ahead of the congregation, creating a structure as I went along. I could see the script in my head and I was in control.

The sermon that arose from the exercise was a drawing together of all the threads that had arisen in the exercise. I was able to respond to the various points different participants had made during the exercise and throw in the odd aside as it occurred to me in that sudden flash of a moment. I was able to move from the main narrative thread of reflections, make apparently obtuse observations and then return to the central message without deviation, repetition or hesitation. In effect, I had become like my parents. I had imbibed their wisdom and learned from their experience and practice and not realised it – until that moment.

Having seen my experiment pay ample dividends, I was determined to try it again. To my delight, it worked even better the second time. From these tentative beginnings has grown a whole approach to preaching. I now possess an array of exercises and participatory games on which to base my preaching. I have used them in many varied settings – from an informal, all-age worship service to a Methodist ordination service. I have found this particular way of 'sharing the Word' to be helpful in assisting people to make links between their everyday experience and the central theological themes in the Christian faith.

Reconnecting to my Black roots by way of a jazz hermeneutic

In more recent times, I have begun to reflect (as scholars are prone to do) upon the very nature of this interactive, extemporised approach to preaching, and have sought to try to find a thematic, theoretical framework in which to house it. What were my familial and community elders doing when they waxed lyrical telling their stories in our front room all those years ago? What am I doing when, drawing on their legacy, I use interactive and participatory exercises in which to construct my approach to 'preaching the Word'?

The answer to some of these questions came when I began to undertake some research for a future book project.[15] Some of the answers I sought were to be found in the practice of jazz music. Jazz is built upon improvisation, and all jazz improvisation is a negotiation between what has been conceived previously and what emerges in that specific moment, either on stage or in the recording studio. All great jazz has its antecedents. To quote a musician friend: 'It all comes from someplace, it isn't entirely yours to make it up as you like, you have a responsibility for this stuff.'

After further consideration, I began to see a clear relationship between jazz music, preaching in general and my preaching in particular.[16] Just as the jazz musician has to respond to the unique context of every performance, bringing new knowledge to life, in the split second of a moment, so too must the preacher. The preacher has to respond to the promptings of the Spirit and the expectations and needs of the congregation. The preacher cannot rely upon what was said the previous week or in a past service – the past in this respect is a foreign country to which there is no return. Even replaying the old sermon, repeating the existing words of the text, is never the same, even second time around. The uniqueness of each occasion demands the freshness of approach and ingenuity of the occasion. The new performance of a piece of music remains connected to past versions of the melody. Whilst the two performances are similar, they are never the same. Similarly, with the preacher, past dramatic perform-ances of the sermon in worship may influence the present, but each new enacted sermon is unique in its own right.

The improvisation of the preacher exists in the interchange between fixity of the text (Scripture) and the fluidity of the con-text (the congregation and the overall worship service). The best preachers are able to apply the text to the context and use the latter to give new life and fresh insight to the former.

Fielding Stewart,[17] Dale Andrews,[18] Carol Tomlin[19] and James Harris[20] have all outlined the differing facets of Black preaching and the relationship between the preacher and the congregation. Within Black oral traditions there exists a togetherness and a con-nectedness between the main or principle speaker and the wider audience or congregation. The meaning and truth of any encounter does not reside solely with the speaker, nor does it lie with the audience. The speaker is not an active force and the congregation or audience a passive one. Conversely, there is an ongoing process of negotiation between the principle speaker and those who are in attendance. The congregation or audience are an active force. Their engagement with the preacher is integral to the successful enactment of the sermon.

Within Black milieus where aspects of Black cultural and religious life are evident, it is not unusual to encounter explicit or implicit examples of a phenomenon many scholars have termed 'Call and Response'. Tomlin defines 'Call and Response' thus: 'In Call-response, the audience responds to the performer, who, in turn, shapes his or her performance according to the audience response. A favourable response will encourage the performer to continue in the same or similar vein; a muted response may suggest a change of course or new strategies.'[21]

Whilst Black preaching comes in many forms and incorporates a wide variety of styles,[22] the expectations placed on Black preachers by their congregations are always high. Preachers are expected to be socially engaged, linking the story of the negated and troubled Black self with the ongoing narrative of redemption and salvation that comes from God's very own self.[23]

The need to bring new meaning and fresh insights from the Bible, whilst remaining connected to the traditions that have informed the collective whole that is 'Holy Scripture', has always been the high challenge presented to Black preachers. It is the challenge to 'bring a fresh word' for the immediate context without doing violence to the text from which one's inspiration is drawn.[24] Essentially, I am arguing that Black preachers within the ongoing dynamic that is Black worship are improvisers, and that improvisation provides a helpful framework for helping us to move beyond the limited binary of evangelical and liberal arguments around biblical authority.

So where am I now?

My journey as a preacher has moved through a number of stages. I have witnessed the oral genius of my elders (particularly my mother) and have imbibed their collective brilliance long before I became a recognised preacher. I have moved from being a compliant White middle-class Methodist wannabe to become a confident and, some might say, loose-cannoned iconoclast. I have developed from being an embarrassed and cowed convention-laden preacher to becoming an interactive, participatory-inspired practitioner.

What has been most important about that journey is the belief that I have found my particular approach. I will not be so arrogant as to term my approach to preaching as unique. Reflecting back on the brilliance that was the Revd Dr William R. Davies in the Eastbrook Hall in Bradford, I witnessed in his preaching glimpses of the method and approach that I would later discover for myself.

As I look back on my development as a preacher I am struck by a number of glaring ironies. I was once a shy, reticent child with a debilitating stutter. Now I am a much-too-wordy extem-porising preacher. (I come from the 'why use one word when five will do' school of preaching.) I was once so shy that I was placed in the 'reticent' group for A- Level English students, as one of the co-teachers despaired of my lack of vocal input in the class. Now ... well, the truth is, I simply love preaching. I know it is godly business, all this preaching stuff, but I would never be so disingenuous as to pretend that a healthy (or, should I say, unhealthy) dose of egoism does not find itself in the business of preaching. I revel in the thrill of standing in front of a con-gregation ready and armed with some participatory exercise, not knowing what will happen next. I have come to learn to trust my improvisatory skills and instincts. I am deeply conscious and proud of the heritage into which I have been nurtured and socialised, and the way in which those resources now inform and influence my approach to preaching.

As a Black theologian and educator, I am firmly of the belief that God has enabled and empowered me to use the creativity and improvisatory skills of my elders in order to preach the Gospel of liberation for all those who need to be released from the structural and systemic sins that besmirch the divine image that resides within them. It has been an enjoyable journey and I thank God for it.

NOTES

1. See Walter Wangerin Jnr, *The Book of God: The Bible as a Novel* (Grand Rapids, Michigan: Zondervan Books, 1996).

2. The official training course for the formation of preachers in Methodism is 'Faith and Worship'. See Connexional Local Preacher's Office at www.methodistchurch.org.uk.

3. See Anthony G. Reddie, *Growing into Hope: Liberation and Change* – Vols 1 & 2 (Peterborough: Methodist Publishing House, 1998) and Anthony G. Reddie, *Nobodies to Somebodies: A Practical Theology for Education and Liberation* (Peterborough: Epworth Press, 2003) for further details on the work of the project.

4. Thomas Groome, *Christian Religious Education* (San Francisco: Harper & Row, 1980), pp. 49–51.

5. Thomas Groome, *Sharing Faith* (San Francisco: Harper, 1991).

6. Ibid., p. 135.

7. In the Christian tradition this is primarily the Bible and the sacred narratives that are contained within it, identified as 'Holy Scripture'.

8. Groome, 1991, pp. 138–51.

9. See Volume 2 of Reddie, *Growing Into Hope*, pp. 7–8.

10. Ibid., pp. 8–9.

11. See Reddie, *Nobodies to Somebodies*, pp.132–40.

12. Groome, 1991, pp. 151–53.

13. Ibid., p. 153.

14. See Anthony G. Reddie, *Faith, Stories and the Experience of Black Elders: Singing the Lord's Song in a Strange Land* (London: Jessica Kingsley, 2001) for an exploration of Black oral tradition and how it can be used as a model for a narrative approach to doing theology.

15. See Anthony G. Reddie, *Inside Looking Out, Outside Looking in: Black Theology in Transatlantic Dialogue* (New York: Palgrave Macmillan, 2006).

16. See Anthony G. Reddie 'Jazz Musicians of the Word', *The Journal of The College of Preachers*, January 2004, pp. 21–28.

17. Carlyle Fielding Stewart, III *Black Spirituality and Black Consciousness* (Trenton, New York: Africa World Press, 1999), pp. 105–120.

18. Dale P. Andrews, *Practical Theology for Black Churches: Bridging Black Theology and African American Folk Religion* (Louisville: John Knox Press, 2002), pp. 16–23.

19. Carol Tomlin, *Black Language Style in Sacred and Secular Contexts* (New York: Caribbean Diaspora Press, 1999), pp. 125–66.
20. James H. Harris, *The Word Made Plain* (Minneapolis: Fortress Press, 2004).
21. Tomlin, op. cit., p. 126.
22. See Joe Aldred (ed.), *Preaching with Power* (London: Cassell, 1998).
23. Ermal Kirby, 'Black Preaching', *The Journal of The College of Preachers* (July 2001), pp. 47–49.
24. Ibid., p.48.

14

Simon Vibert

A HIGH CALLING –
CONVERSION AND
COMMISSION

Simon Vibert was born in 1963 and was ordained in 1989. He has served as a curate in Carlisle, was Minister in Charge of Trinity Church, Buxton and for the last six years has been Vicar of St Luke's, Wimbledon Park. He is the author of a forthcoming book on Christian marriage. He holds an M.Th. from Glasgow University and a D.Min. from Reformed Theological Seminary, Orlando. He is married to Carrie and they have three children.

When I was a boy, sermons were associated with incredible boredom and abject irrelevance. I can remember spending many Sunday mornings in the choir stall of my local Anglican church. One way to while away what seemed like hours, was to count the number of times our bumbling vicar 'erred'! We passed notes along the choir stalls and spent our time adding up the hymn numbers on the board to see which week had the highest total.

With youthful irreverence, it seemed to us that our vicar had mastered the art of speaking for a long time without actually saying anything.

Many of my views of preaching were shaped by this popular perception. It was not until I left this particular church and our family joined another local Anglican church where the vicar, a family friend, had recently been installed that my views changed. He was self-confessedly disorganised and prepared many of his sermons as he climbed the pulpit steps. I often wondered what the effect of increasing the height of the pulpit might have had upon his preaching! He was a very caring man and occasionally shared some very insightful things. In fact, my memories of him have more to do with his desire to encourage me as a preacher than anything that he said.

At the age of seventeen I was a very new convert. I think that, largely through that vicar and a couple of other friends, I pretty much welcomed the Gospel when I first heard it. It was a blessed relief from the formal liberalism with which I had been brought up and which left me laden with guilt and feeling that I must 'try harder'.

The Gospel, on the other hand, came as a tremendous relief! No longer did I need to try to make myself acceptable – and I wanted the world to know it. I wanted to preach! For me, there was never a separate 'call to ministry'. I just assumed that anyone who had come to faith would be equally desperate to tell others about it at every opportunity. My poor family got the leftovers of my enthusiasm over meal times.

A favourite text was Philippians 1:21. 'For me to live is Christ, to die is gain!' I passionately believed it (and still do). Here at last was something to live for, something to die for. Finally, something had motivated me to think, to learn, to study and to have a focus for my idleness.

My new vicar was keen to encourage me to preach and he gave me my first opportunity as a very new Christian. I wrote the sermon out long-hand and practised it in front of the mirror. I reckoned it took about 15 minutes. Come Sunday, I read through my notes rather hastily in my nervousness. It was over in five minutes, so I decided to turn the page over and do it all again, and sat down after nine minutes!

Now, as a vicar of a local congregation, I often think about how careful I am about 'guarding the pulpit', but I am grateful to have had the opportunity to preach at a young age. I am very aware too that, for all his foibles, my vicar had seen in me what I hadn't yet even seen in myself: a call to preach.

The old saying is a great encouragement to me: 'God had only one Son and he made him a preacher!' Indeed, as John tells us: 'No one has ever seen God, but God the One and Only, who is at the Father's side, has made him known' (John 1:18). In Johannine theology, the eternal Son, the second person of the Trinity, is introduced as the Word. God's self-expression is in the form of word, yes, word made flesh, but nevertheless word. And he has made him known – or has 'exegeted' the Father.

What a high calling! He has entrusted preachers with the daunting task of following in the Son's footsteps. 'These are written that you may believe that Jesus is the Christ, the Son of God, and that by believing you may have life in his name' (John 20:31). We preachers share with the apostolic role : 'we proclaim to you the eternal life, which was with the Father and has appeared to us. We proclaim to you what we have seen and heard, so that you also may have fellowship with us' (1 John 1:2b, 3a).

A formative year – learning to love the Word

A high calling indeed! But I was very aware of how 'green' I was. As a new Christian, I was painfully aware of my ignorance. I felt myself very fortunate that my church warden was also my careers master at school. How many people have their careers teacher praying for their pupil's future ministry? Through a friend of his in the City, I ended up as 'the Slave' at St Helen's Church, Bishopsgate.[1]

I had never heard until then of Dick Lucas, let alone the

amazing lunchtime work and training ministry based in St Helen's in the heart of London's square mile. Rather arrogantly, I can remember saying to myself: 'If I can learn the Bible through this man, I shall listen to him.' It was a test which Dick Lucas would unfailingly pass, of course.

Dick's supreme ability is to enable the hearer to go away from the sermon and to hear the message of the passage. I can remember him taking the most famous verse of the Bible, from John 3:16: 'For God so loved the world that he gave his one and only Son, that whoever believes in him shall not perish but have eternal life.' Many preachers, myself included, find that preaching on the most familiar passages can often be the hardest. What can you say that the congregation has not already heard? But decades later I can still recall Dick saying words to the effect that: 'This is probably the most famous verse in the Bible, but the problem is, we don't believe it, do we? No longer do we believe that Jesus is God's one and only Son. No longer do we believe that if you don't believe in him, you will perish.' Just by coming at the text from another angle, he made those old truths come home with fresh force and power, as we saw how the impact of modern challenges over the uniqueness of Christ and the reality of eternal punishment are addressed by this ancient text.

Whilst in later years Dick was to form the Proclamation Trust – a marvellous aid to clear biblical preaching that has influenced many evangelical pastors, possibly more than any other theological education – I learned more about preaching from hearing him do it, weekly at the Tuesday lunchtime service and on Sundays. It is often the case that those who preach well, whilst they can explain what they do to prepare and deliver their sermons, still do not exhaust the marvel of hearing them actually do it.

I was also very struck by some of his preaching habits. After the Tuesday lunchtime meeting I would have the task of stacking chairs, tidying away books and generally clearing up the church. I would often go into the pulpit and retrieve Dick's notes and Bible. Learning from his notes never helped me much – I couldn't possibly read his writing! However, I do recall taking them into his study for him, and being surprised that he ripped them up and hurled them into the waste paper basket! It was a great lesson in the need to prepare afresh each time one preaches. I was also very struck by the way in which Dick would often preach and repreach the same passage until he felt that he had got it clear in his mind.

I know that he would blush at my sincere admiration for him, but I do think that I owe more to Dick's preaching than almost anything else subsequently. I often read a passage and can hear a Dick Lucas sermon in the back of my mind as I prepare my own sermons.

Formal education – a hunger for truth

Academically, I was a very late starter. At the end of winter term, the year of my O Levels, it looked like I was going to crash out of school. Nothing motivated me for study – even the financial inducements my father tried! The carrot was too far in the future. Then, in the first year of the sixth form, I became a Christian. All of a sudden I had a motivation to study. Life had a meaning and a purpose. Of course, it takes more than three years in the sixth form to make up for five years of idleness! However, the appetite was there, at last. My mind was now opening, not just to spiritual realities, but with a general hunger and motivation for living. Yes, for me, to live is Christ!

In my early twenties I was accepted as an ordinand in the Church of England. At first, Oak Hill Theological College in North London was an eye-opener for me. I enjoyed the academic study. This was my first degree, and I had quite a lot of catching up to do.

Things have changed quite a bit at Oak Hill now, but at the time, I was surprised to find that there was no homiletics course. The danger with my preaching was that sermons turned into essays. Too much was crammed into the sermon and the congregation must have suffered with spiritual indigestion! I was torn much of the time, because the teenage models of preaching I had been brought up with had left me feeling hungry and unsatisfied. Consequently, I often counterbalanced by putting too much in my sermons. After ordination, I opted for a Doctor of Ministry degree, and a memorable class for me was one taught by Dr Richard Pratt on the whole post-modern environment in which we minister. People are suspicious of truth claims and this is quite a challenge for the preacher. He also warned, though, of the danger of assuming that modernity is right. Many of us have been brought up with a 'John Wayne' style of preaching, whereby the lone hero rides into town with truth on his side, shooting down every doctrinal error, and this is often manifested in a didactic, logical synergistic style of preaching. As the old preacher joke goes: 'My job is to speak; your job is to listen. If you feel that you have finished your job before I have finished mine, please try to be patient with me.' It isn't only in the dictionary that monologue and monotony find themselves side by side!

Preaching as bridge-building

I don't consider myself to be an academic theologian, although I am often criticised for preaching sermons which are 'too academic'. This is not always my fault, for we live in a peculiarly anti-intellectual age. Preaching is thought to be worthwhile only when the sermon speaks to 'me and my need, in the here and now', whereas the biblical themes are much wider than that. However, I realise that often my preaching is abstract and unearthed, and it is only the power of the story which enlivens and makes it real.

The bigger temptation is to give up on preaching altogether. In part, this is because of the sheer busyness of parish life. Sermon preparation is hard work and it requires time. How easy, it seems, it is to fill one's week with everything else! However, the more subtle temptation to give up on preaching is one which I think the Apostle Paul hints at in Romans 1:16: 'I am not ashamed of the Gospel, because it is the power of God for the salvation of

everyone who believes, first for the Jew, then for the Gentile.'
Would the mighty apostle have written these words if he had not
felt the temptation to be ashamed?

How often the devil whispers in the preacher's ear, 'You've got
nothing! Do you really think that this message will change lives?'
But the Gospel is the power of God for salvation. God has said
that 'anyone who trusts in him will never be put to shame'
(Romans 10:11). So, Paul goes on: 'How, then, can they call on the
one they have not believed in? And how can they believe in the
one of whom they have not heard? And how can they hear
without someone preaching to them?' (Romans 10:14). One
analogy which I have often used is the idea that preaching is
rather like eating. It is not for nothing that Jesus refuted the
devil's temptation with the words 'Man does not live on bread
alone, but on every word that comes from the mouth of God'.
And the more one eats, the more one's appetite grows. Not only
should we long to be fed by the Word, but our palate and
appreciation for the fine, mature food of the Word should grow. I
remember sitting on a bus and watching a long-suffering mother
placate her bawling baby. She patiently removed a Farley's rusk
from her bag. In my pre-parenting days, all I could think of doing
would be to ram that thing in the toothy hole and plug the noise!
Being far wiser than I, she put the rusk in the baby's hand and
allowed the child to raise it to its mouth. Nobody likes having
'the Bible rammed down their throats' by overzealous preachers.
Rather, the great challenge is to put an open book in people's
hands so that they may feed themselves.

In recent years I have benefited greatly from the preaching of
Dr John Piper, pastor of Bethlehem Baptist Church in
Minneapolis. He has memorably encouraged us to make God the
centre of our worship. God is to be our delight! For the sake of
joy, we forsake all other pleasures in this life. His provocative
comment about Christian hedonism, namely that the 'chief end
of man is to glorify God by enjoying him forever' has led me to a
fresh exploration of Jonathan Edwards, the great New England
Revivalist preacher of the mid eighteenth century.[2]

What Edwards, and subsequently Piper, have taught me is that the Word has not done its work until it has been applied to the heart or the affections. Hence, Edwards says: 'The religion which God requires, and will accept, does not consist in weak, dull and lifeless wishes, raising us but a little above a state of indifference: God, in His word, greatly insists upon it, that we be in good earnest, "fervent in spirit," and our hearts vigorously engaged in religion …'[3]

It was said of Jonathan Edwards that he 'had the power of presenting an argument and with such intenseness of feeling, that the whole soul of the speaker is thrown into every part of the conception and delivery; so that the solemn attention of the whole audience is riveted, from the beginning to the close, and impressions are left that cannot be effaced'.[4]

John Piper, in *The Supremacy of God in Preaching*, says that the vision of Isaiah 6 is our goal every Sunday: through preaching we unveil the glory of God for our hearers. The goal of preaching is therefore nothing less than heightening our God-consciousness, so that we come to worship God with heart, soul, mind and strength.

Conclusion

As far as my story goes, it has been a growing appetite for God's Word, with a desire to feed others. But this has, all along the way, been shaped and moulded by people who have invested in my life, either in their pulpit ministry, or in their encouragement.

This relationship between the eternal Word and living Christians shapes my attitude to the week-in-week-out sermon preparation with which I am involved. For me, there is a direct relationship between three things. 'Seeing it done well' makes me want to emulate good preachers. Hearing challenging and con-victing truth from the Scriptures is enlivened by people who 'get on and live and do it'! And, finally, time spent labouring over the text, ruminating and masticating on the Word, results in an over-whelming desire to let the Word out to do its own work.

God, then, is the only audience which matters. And Paul's strong words of encouragement motivate me to simplicity, intensity and integrity in this role: 'Since, then, we know what it is to fear the Lord, we try to persuade men. What we are is plain to God, and I hope it is also plain to your conscience ... We are therefore Christ's ambassadors, as though God were making his appeal through us. We implore you on Christ's behalf: be reconciled to God.' (2 Cor. 5:11, 20).

This is a great privilege and a high calling.

NOTES

1. An affectionate title for the menial but privileged role we 'slaves' undertook in helping with the practicalities of midweek lunchtime services.

2. See John Piper, *Desiring God. Meditations of a Christian Hedonist* (Portland, Oregon, USA: Multnomah Press, 1996).

3. Jonathan Edwards, *The Religious Affections* (Edinburgh: Banner of Truth Trust, 1994), p. 27.

4. John Piper, *The Supremacy of God in Preaching* (Leicester: Inter-Varsity Press, 1990).

15
David Wilkinson

MISTAKES, FAILURES AND
THE CONFIDENCE
OF OTHERS

David Wilkinson is a Methodist minister, recently appointed as the Principal of St John's College in the University of Durham. As well as an MA in Theology from the University of Cambridge, he has completed two PhDs: the first in Theoretical Astrophysics in 1987, and more recently a PhD in Systematic Theology. David was a chaplain at Liverpool University, and his wife, Alison, is also a Methodist minister.

My journey to the pulpit has been characterised by mistakes, failures and the unbelievable confidence of others. In fact, my first ever sermon combined all three!

After having made a significant Christian commitment just a few months earlier, I joined my college Christian Union in my first year at Durham University. As I was the only person who joined in my year, when it came to asking people to lead the CU group I was the only first-year available. I struggled to know what to do with a group of what seemed to me much older spiritual superstars but they were very encouraging and supportive. This was especially the case when I faced my first 'Outside Activity', which was an occasion when the group went to lead worship in a church in the region. So encouraging and supportive in fact, that although I asked at least ten people to preach the sermon they all had good reasons not to. Unanimously they thought I should do it. I suspect this had more to do with them wanting a free weekend rather than a word from the Lord that I was especially gifted in this area.

Eventually there was no one else to ask. I was in a panic because I didn't have the first idea of what to do. However, I was reading a book of sermons at the time by the Baptist preacher Alan Redpath. They were really speaking to me and the solution seemed simple. I was sure Dr Redpath would not mind me 'borrowing' one of his sermons in such a situation of need for the Gospel. So I copied out one of his sermons and translated it into my own words. I added a few illustrations to personalise it and this at least stopped the immediate panic.

I tried it through a few times and the 35-minute length did not worry me. After all, we had been told it was a small congregation of ten old ladies. When we arrived at the church the ten elderly ladies were there, but no one had told us that it was Parade Sunday and that the ladies were to be joined by some fifty small children in the form of Scouts and Brownies. I should have adapted my sermon, of course. But panic set in again and I could not think of anything else to do but preach the prepared sermon. So that is what I did.

I felt things had gone reasonably well until on the way back to college one of my friends said, 'What did you think of that little boy?' 'What little boy?' I replied. 'The little boy,' he said, 'who stood up halfway through your sermon and shouted out "How much longer is he going on for?"' I had been so nervous that the boy's intervention on behalf of the congregation had completely passed me by.

That first sermon sums up much of my pulpit journey of the

next twenty years, including no doubt countless numbers of people who have silently wondered just how long I would be going on for. Most of my steps forward on the journey have occurred through 'borrowing' from my preaching heroes or by being thrust into situations which were a little beyond me.

Borrowing from heroes

My preaching heroes have been the source for inspiration, models and occasionally content. The first real Bible exposition I ever heard was soon after I became a Christian. The Anglican teacher and evangelist David Watson was giving a series of talks on discipleship at the Greenbelt Arts Festival. I couldn't believe just how exciting listening to one person speak could be. I found God speaking to me powerfully. I bought the audio tapes and listened again and again. Alongside the challenge to discipleship, I began to notice the method he was using. It was a simple structure – big headline point, biblical verse, illustration, application, next big headline point and so on. I also noticed the way he told jokes, his timing with a big audience, and the amount of his own experience he used. At the same time I was reading and listening to Alan Redpath, learning the way that Scripture was immediately applied to the heart of my spiritual life. We were also fortunate to have Donald English, the Methodist leader and theologian, as a family friend. His tapes were around my parents' house and whenever he preached in the north-east of England we would go to hear him. With Donald, Scripture was brought alive 'in conversation with' the reality of the contemporary world. With all of these preachers you were introduced to the scriptures through their personality, with a deep, sympathetic understanding of human frailty and an excitement with Jesus.

So that was why, when I started preaching, I modelled myself on these preachers. I followed their structures, used their applications of biblical verses, and mimicked their delivery. This gave me a little bit of confidence during the panic and nervousness of trying to preach. Indeed, at this stage I was being asked to preach at student and church groups but without any formal training or indeed without any mentoring. I needed to know whether I was doing it right. I sensed an enjoyment in preaching but I also felt the responsibility. At that stage I naively believed that every member of the congregation was inwardly digesting each one of my words and I did not want to lead people astray. Later I would learn the reality of people's engagement with the sermon, but I still feel the responsibility. I do not want to cause people to stumble on their own faith journey and I want God to use the spoken word of the sermon for his glory.

Soon I did receive that training and mentoring from the structure of Methodist local preaching, but most of my learning has come from observing other preachers. I will never be able to craft a sermon as beautifully as David Day, but I can learn much from his use of language, humour and his approach to Scripture. I could never preach like Eric Delve, but the clarity of presenting the challenge of the Gospel will always be at the back of my mind. I marvel at the depth of exposition in the sermons of Martyn Lloyd-Jones, finding that the lectionary of Bible passages that I most often use does not allow a preacher to spend several years going through Romans! I read books of sermons rather than Bible study notes for my daily quiet times and, while a student, loved the Saturday evening Bible expositions in the Christian Union where I heard many of the leading UK preachers.

You will notice that up to this point my role models are very White and very male. Indeed, as a student I went through a phase of believing that there was nothing wrong with that, because God only called men to preach and Western evangelicalism was as close to the New Testament as anything could be. The Lord, of course, has a sense of humour in these things, and I now find myself married to one the finest preachers I know. Alison sees different things in the text from what I see. She uses very different illustrations and has a very different approach to preaching. She also sees very different ways of applying the text. As I have listened to her and other female preachers I have learned an immense amount. I am beginning to discover just how narrow my approach to Scripture, my application and illustrative material can be. I also see people relating to her preaching in a way that they do not connect to mine. This has had an immense effect on my preaching.

Furthermore, I have encountered preachers from different cultures, such as Mvume Dandala, now the General Secretary of the African Council of Churches, who have reminded me just how blinkered Western evangelicalism can be. Mvume preaches with a joy that is often rare in White Western male preaching, and sees in the Scriptures evangelism alongside issues of social justice, so often kept apart in Western Christianity.

Now it is fair to say that I initially struggled with this. After all, my assessment of whether someone was a good preacher and whether or not they could teach me anything was based largely on whether they already preached like me. Preachers from different styles, cultures or theologies sounded strange and threatening. Of course, there are questions of what is good and bad preaching, but my feelings in this area were often dominated by my basic insecurity in my own faith and pulpit journey. As I have put more of my confidence in the Lord, I feel less threatened that those who preach in a different way from me mean that my approach is wrong. I am learning to value other styles and I value learning from those other styles.

It is interesting that as I look back over twenty years of preaching, I have never had a close mentor who has 'discipled' me in preaching. I am convinced that the key to development on the pulpit journey is giving the preacher confidence. I found it initially by relying on my heroes. Others will find it in a more personal relationship. Confidence is of such importance if I am going to preach in the first place and then if I am going to try new things in preaching. This should not be an arrogant self-importance but an inner confidence that God will use this weak failure of a Christian in preaching his Word.

At this point in my own pulpit journey, I therefore wonder whether I am a good model for others. I find myself teaching classes on preaching and preaching at events where there are lots of other preachers present. Does my approach give confidence? That is, do I give enough encouragement and confidence to those who are starting to preach, not that they become clones of my approach, but that they can emerge as preachers with their own gifts and passions? This challenges me to a faithful and imaginative engagement with Scripture, but also to an openness to let other preachers see the 'real me'. I recall clearing up the room at the end of a very powerful evangelistic message given by a famous preacher. I noticed that the speaker had left his notes at the front, and I could not stop myself from looking at the notes of this man to see how he had constructed them. But right at the top of page one was scrawled in large letters 'REMEMBER TO BUY MILK BEFORE COMING HOME TONIGHT'. It may not have taught me much about sermon construction but it reminded me of the importance of our humanity!

However, I also realise that throughout my pulpit journey I will not be a good model for everyone. For the Church to develop new preachers, there needs to be a variety of models. I wonder, therefore, whether there is enough diversity amongst our leading preachers. Although there has been some progress, many high-profile UK Christian services, events and conferences are dominated by middle-aged, or elderly, White men. How, for example, are young women preachers going to develop if they cannot see women role models being given the chance at major events and conferences?

Unbelievable risk

In addition to my heroes, there have been others who have been important on my pulpit journey. These are the people who have taken huge risks in giving me a pulpit to preach from. This never ceases to amaze me. I remember standing in front of 5000 international leaders at the World Methodist Conference, about to give the keynote address, and thinking to myself that none of the organising committee had ever heard me speak before! They were taking a huge risk and yet it opened up a new phase of ministry for me. If they had minimised the risk I should have been asked to do only the opening prayer, but they saw the importance of giving someone younger the chance to speak.

In a similar way, the evangelist Rob Frost gave me opportunities for preaching and Bible exposition at large Christian gatherings when I was young and virtually without experience. He could have insisted that only well-known names were invited to preach, but he gave me the opportunity. These were times of real challenge for me, where my trust in God deepened and my calling as a preacher was confirmed.

Not only did it involve risk on the part of others, it also involved gifted preachers standing aside in order to give me an opportunity. This takes a great deal of humility and a commitment to seeing others developing in their pulpit journey. The most recent part of my pulpit journey has shown me just how hard that is.

As a Methodist minister in Liverpool in the 1990s, I had pastoral charge of one church. We experienced by God's grace significant growth, not least in the area of people receiving the call to preach. At one stage we had 24 lay preachers in a church of around 200 people. While in the Methodist system they could preach in other churches in the Circuit of churches, they also wanted, of course, the opportunity to preach at their home church. However, each Sunday we had only three services rather than 24. I found myself increasingly having to take a back seat in order to give these new preachers opportunity to preach.

I found this extremely difficult as, after all, my main gift was preaching. God had called me to be a preacher and that is what I did for a large part of my living. In fact, my self-identity within the ministry was largely invested in my role as a preacher. Now I was having to make space for people to preach who were not as good or as experienced as I was! I worried about the bad theology the congregation would experience from these young preachers and I worried about what some of these preachers wore. After all, could you really preach good news dressed in a

Preston North End football shirt and a baseball cap? Most of all, I worried that the congregation would complain that I was not working hard enough for the money they were paying me.

God had to teach me many things during that time. Some suggested that the new preachers should only get the opportunity to preach at our smaller services. Yet it seemed to me that they needed to preach at the large main service as well as in front of smaller groups if they were really going to learn. Others suggested that some of those called to preach were not mature enough as Christians to have this responsibility. When a fourteen-year-old came to see me to tell me he felt God calling him to preach, I myself had the same kinds of reservation. However, I could not forget that people had taken risks with me.

It is a testimony to the maturity of the congregation that so many of these young preachers have gone forward into key Christian leadership. A few have dropped out, but the majority are still growing as preachers. Eleven men and women have gone on to be church leaders in Methodist and Anglican churches alone, while the fourteen-year-old was recently awarded the top First in Theology at Oxford and is now emerging as one of our brightest preachers and theologians.

The challenge to my pulpit journey was the need to see my own gift and calling in preaching as part of a team of preachers who brought diversity to the experience of encountering Scripture. Too often I have been too individualistic in understanding God's call, and preaching itself has a tendency to emphasise that. I am more and more convinced that a church will not grow in maturity unless it has a team of preachers of different ages, genders and backgrounds. Now, of course, there have been churches which have grown under the preaching ministry of one person. But I believe that these are remarkable exceptions rather than recipes for growing churches. Strong and charismatic leadership is important, but how that leadership encourages others is the key beyond simple numeric growth of a local church, that is the sending out of disciples in new areas of mission and ministry. Furthermore, can I take risks with others in the same way that God has taken a risk with me?

In addition, the congregation of a church need to take the long-term view and not complain too much that they do not hear enough of 'their minister' if other preachers are going to develop on their own journey. They too need to take risks. I find it often the case that congregations are better at doing this than their ministers!

Being taught by the congregation

This leads me on to think more about the major influence various congregations have been on my preaching journey. Feedback, including the shouting of small boys, has helped me enormously.

At this point I need to confess that my natural tendency is to run away from feedback. I struggle still with standing at the door at the end of a service, fearful of what people will say. I find it hard when they say nice things, I find it hard when they say critical things, I find it even harder when they say nothing at all, or the standard 'Nice hymns'. Nevertheless over years of preaching to the same congregation, they feed you so much. You think through sermons in relation to the real people you know will be there. An encouraging congregation who are hungry to hear God's Word is a great privilege.

I therefore owe a great deal to Elm Hall Drive Methodist Church in Liverpool where I was their minister, because they taught me how to preach. I remember the businessman who, after what I thought was a great sermon on love, asked me how he was going to show love to the people he had been forced to make redundant in order to save the business. I remember the long discussion over coffee, after another 'great' sermon on the spiritual lessons from the book of Jonah, on the topic of whether or not the whale story was actually true. I remember the annual list which was passed to me of what the children in the church liked and disliked about worship. My talks featured often in these lists and you can imagine under which category!

These forms of feedback caused me to reassess what I was doing. My staff team at Elm Hall Drive also helped me during our Monday morning meetings and gently pointed out areas to be worked on. Some preachers set up more formal structures for feedback, but I have mainly worked with congregations and colleagues who have done much of this informally.

Part of the key to this feedback is that it has been mostly given in the form of encouragement when I have done something good, rather than criticism when I have got it wrong. The BBC TV series *Little Angels* gives advice to parents on how to look after difficult toddlers. An important principle is to be very strong on encouragement when a child is good and try to ignore the child if he or she is being naughty to gain attention. Although the parallel between me as a preacher and a small child is not strictly accurate, I do respond in exactly the same way to encouragement. My staff colleagues would encourage me when things had gone well and stay oddly silent at other times! My wife has been a constant source of encouraging feedback. The congregation in Liverpool were also very generous in words of encouragement.

Of course the congregation also show you God at work. William Barclay once said 'there is no greater joy than leading someone to Christ'. To see individuals respond to the preached word and grow in discipleship is about joy. It is also a reminder of how the amazing grace of God can take our weakness, bad preparation and inability to pronounce Old Testament names and use them. There is always a tension between professionalism and weakness in the preaching task. I want to hone this gift and develop my artistry as a preacher. Indeed, I believe that I am called by God to do this. At the same time the tendency to trust in self rather than in the Spirit is always there.

Foolishness and forgiveness

This is where mistakes and failures become important. I still remember the fiasco of my first sermon with shivers down my spine. Yet I also remember it with thankfulness and amazement.

After such an experience, why did the pulpit journey continue? It has to be something to do with God rather than me.

Very early in my preaching journey I felt God calling me to be an evangelist. It was an extremely clear call, not something that I usually experience. Reading John's gospel, the verse 'You did not choose me but I chose you and appointed you that you go and bear fruit' jumped out of the Bible and hit me square between the eyes. I knew what it was about. God was saying to me that he would bring fruit in terms of new Christians as a result of my preaching, it was so clear to me that I believed it. I thanked God and when appropriate began to invite people at the end of certain sermons to come forward as a sign of a commitment or recommitment.

The only trouble was that I gave those invitations for five years before anyone responded. I looked foolish on a number of occasions, and was well aware of voices saying 'he's getting carried away with himself'. I look back at that time, remembering the embarrassment of no one responding. I had said my prayers, was trying to be faithful to God's call and did everything to try to preach in a way that would allow people to encounter God. Yet there were lessons during that time I needed to learn. Now when I preach and people respond, I know that they respond not because of me but because of the Lord at work in them. It was a hard lesson but it was important for me and I am thankful.

At times I have fallen over on my journey to the pulpit – literally! I have preached the same sermon twice to the same congregation by mistake; I wish I could say that they noticed! I have been heckled, tut-tutted and have had things thrown at me. I have preached theology which I now regret, and have made a huge number of insensitive statements, offending many people – just how many I will never know. I have been sexist, ageist and racist and misrepresented the Word of God.

It is at this point that I note I would no longer be on this pulpit journey if I did not follow a God who offers forgiveness, a new start and the power to transform lives. As I encounter that God in Jesus I get the chance to say sorry and to begin again. Indeed, my love of Jesus is stronger now than ever, as is my joy at being called to be a preacher. Of course I do not bound enthusiastically into every pulpit, especially in those churches which should have been closed twenty years ago and think only of themselves rather than God's mission. Sometimes the preparation is hard and the sense of responsibility is frightening. Nevertheless it is what I have been called to do, and as I preach I sense the presence and power of the Lord.

Alan Redpath would often preface his sermons by saying that it is a great feeling for a preacher to look at a passage in the Bible, break it into different parts and put it back together in a skilful way as preparation to preaching it. But, it is even better when the passage breaks the preacher apart and then skilfully puts the preacher back together in preparation for the sermon. I have felt that. My joy at approaching Scripture to prepare a sermon has been because of the way in which during the preaching preparation and the event God has spoken to me.

It never ceases to amaze me that God speaks and that he is indeed prepared to take unbelievable risks with people like me by involving them in the preaching ministry. Behind the confidence of others who have helped me on my pulpit journey, and through all the mistakes and the failures, has been the confidence of the Lord. I guess that's grace.